BAD (Begin Again Differently)

ADVANCE PRAISE

"Claudette provides an inspirational reflection and pragmatic roadmap that is useful for anyone looking for a way to recover from a significant setback."

—Matthew J. Pepper, Ed.D.

"Claudette inspires you to fail into your success by transforming old patterns within yourself. Her book will help people to change their circumstances in order to reach new levels in business or personal endeavors. You will ultimately accomplish your purpose of producing what you expect to result every day!"

—Sabrenay Brandon, YES, INC. Team Member

"I encourage every reader to communicate with Claudette and to share your own stories and endeavors. I believe that regardless of the products or services being offered, the strength of her messages in BAD will work for anyone. Any organization will benefit from her 7 smart processes to begin again differently, better, stronger, and more effectively."

—*The Late Margaret Jorgensen, Ph.D.*

BEGIN AGAIN DIFFERENTLY

7 SMART PROCESSES to Win Again After Suffering a Business Loss

CLAUDETTE YARBROUGH

NEW YORK

LONDON • NASHVILLE • MELBOURNE • VANCOUVER

BAD (Begin Again Differently)

7 Smart Processes to Win Again After Suffering a Business Loss

© 2020 Claudette Yarbrough

Published in New York, New York, by Morgan James Publishing in partnership with Difference Press. Morgan James is a trademark of Morgan James, LLC.
www.MorganJamesPublishing.com

ISBN 9781631950568 paperback
ISBN 9781631950575 eBook
ISBN 9781631952081 audiobook
Library of Congress Control Number: 2020933034

Cover Design Concept:
Jennifer Stimson

Cover Design by:
Jonathan Lewis,
jonathan@jonlincreative.com

Interior Design by:
Christopher Kirk
www.GFSstudio.com

Editor:
Cory Hott

Book Coaching:
The Author Incubator

Morgan James is a proud partner of Habitat for Humanity Peninsula and Greater Williamsburg. Partners in building since 2006.

Get involved today! Visit
MorganJamesPublishing.com/giving-back

This book is dedicated to first of all, my mother, Minnie Lee Higgs, because one day she turned her life over to God, and my sisters and I have never the same after that. Secondly to my son, Benjamin, because he is the best son a mom could ever ask for and finally to God who has given me many experiences and caused me to meet many people over the course of my life that have caused me to become the person who wrote this book.

TABLE OF CONTENTS

FOREWORD

little over a year ago, I was living in Buffalo, NY. A place I called home for my entire life. I was working two full-time jobs with a master's degree, trying to keep up with life. My debts were mounting, and I found myself living to work. There were many days when I could not tell when my day was beginning or ending. I could not think because I did not have time. I was too busy, let alone able to find time for much else. There were so many days when my workday would start at 7:00 AM and it would not finish until 2:30 AM. I would travel from one job to the next, with twenty minutes in-between to stop by a drive-thru window. After work, if I was lucky, I had just enough time to sleep for a few hours, maybe eat a little something, and take a shower to refresh myself before repeating the same process of work each day. Time off for me was a rare occasion. I had earned plenty of it, but I was so busy working, I did not have time, nor did I understand the concept of taking a break. I did not even take any time off from work when my father passed away. I am sure many of you have found yourself in a similar position once or twice.

For fifteen years, I worked for a not for profit agency in Buffalo, NY providing services to persons with intellectual disabilities and mental illness. I was in charge of the oversight and management of multiple residential and day habilitation services throughout my tenure. I was in charge of not only the daily monitoring and oversight, but also the supervision, hiring, and oversight of employees who worked in the programs I was leading. I was directly responsible for multiple 24/7 operations. As you can imagine, this was not always the easiest job, and it required a tremendous amount of carefully thought out strategic planning. My role could not be taken lightly because other people's lives were at stake. It was a huge responsibility, but I loved my job and I loved the people I served. Everything was always about serving others. I put so much love into the work that I was doing, that eventually it burned me out. I was the typical person who loved to please. I was so busy working that I did not have time to stop and think, let alone stop to reflect on what I was doing or why I was doing. I did not know any better. All I knew was that I was responsible, and I had big shoes to fill.

Just like a fire without a fuel source, I burned out. I was exhausted. I was so tired of working two jobs, trying to manage all of these people and things, trying to pay off my mounting debts and taking care of my mother who suffers from several debilitating and ongoing medical conditions that I started to lack passion. I began to lose focus, and I had lost sight of the things that really mattered. I struggled daily to get up, get dressed, and go to work. I remember breaking down in tears often because I was trying my best but feeling my worst. After several conversations with my significant other, I finally decided that it was time to make a change.

It did not take me long after that to set my plan for change in motion. Although it was a difficult decision, and I would encounter many speed bumps along the way. I turned in my resignation, and, I listed my mother's house for sale. I terminated the lease on our apartment, sold many of our belongings including two vehicles and we called my husband's parents to assist us in locating a new place to live 1550 miles away in San Antonio, Texas.

A few months later, I put my mother on a plane and we packed up two households and drove across the country in our U-hauls with our remaining vehicles in tow. I began the process of starting over. It took several months to adjust to our new surroundings and to re-establish new medical providers. In my downtime, I took a much-needed break! For me, this was not an easy adjustment. I did not even know how to take a break, I found myself looking for things to keep me busy. Eventually, my savings were depleted, and I needed to start looking for a new job. At first, I reached out and applied to positions in the same field. I went to a few interviews and received a few offers, but something inside of me was telling me not to take that same path. I struggled with myself because I loved that field but somehow that field just did not love me back in a way that was healthy.

I continued to explore. I came across a listing online for a job in my community that really compelled me to apply. This may sound cliché, but I feel as though a higher power called me to this opportunity and therefore, I applied. Have you ever decided to do something just because something from within you was calling you to it? That was me! I almost lost hope along the way because the process took longer than I had ever experienced, however, as soon as I stopped worrying, the call came through. I was notified that I was selected as a finalist for the position, and I was asked to meet and interview with the CEO of YES Inc., Ms. Claudette Yarbrough.

I knew right when I met Ms. Yarbrough for the first time, that I had found a new calling. She had something to offer me shortly after that meeting, but it was not only a job that she was offering me, it was an opportunity to change. Everything about the position I was hired for was vastly different than anything I had ever done. In fact, I had asked the question, "What a typical day might look like for me?" Ms. Yarbrough said, "I can't answer that for you, everything is different, and every day is new." One of the first things her team members had communicated with me was that if I were going to be successful, I would need to be able to "embrace change" and "to trust the process." At first, I did not fully understand what was meant by "trust the process" but I soon came to understand that I needed to believe in what I was doing and everything that is done or asked of me, is done with purpose. The second thing I was told to do was to be purposeful about keep and reflecting in a daily journal. I had never really written in a journal consistently and I thought at first, what an odd way to conduct business, and why would this be a good use of my time. I soon realized that the journal I was keeping was the key to my growth and success. I filled my first 168-sheet front and back hardcover journal up in less than a month. I am still amazed at what I was able to learn and accomplish within just a few weeks. I have always had confidence, but it is really something when you find out that you do not know all there is to know about yourself. It is an expectation that I write in my journal each day. I have made a habit of writing in my journal now, not because it is expected, but because it has become a part of me and has made me more effective in all areas of my life.

After being introduced to her organization's mission, vision, and core values, I was quickly able to align myself with the noble goal. Having a noble goal is highly important to being success-ful. When you have a noble goal, you want to ensure that every-thing you do in life is aligning with that goal. When you know why you are doing it, it becomes easier to get it done. I remem-ber when I was younger, my mother used to call me the "why child". I was always asking my mom "why" most of the time, I ended up hearing "because I said so" after I asked her several why is in one conversation. I have always been concerned with the "why" behind the motive to do, or not to do. When you know why it becomes easier to understand the purpose. When I grew up and life happened, somehow, I stopped asking why, because I thought it did not matter so much, and I really did not think I had time to continue to ask "why." I realized after meeting Ms. Yar-brough, and having the time provided to do that type of thinking, that it is important. It is also important to make sure your goals and your "why" aligns. When you are in alignment, it is easier to be the same person at work, as you are at home and in the community. It is possible to be one whole person, instead of being one way while at work and being another when you are at home. When you are not in alignment with your noble goal, you will find yourself off track. Ms. Yarbrough instilled the importance of setting and writing goals not just for the company, but also for ourselves. When we are able to write our goals down, it gives us a way to hold ourselves accountable for the work and effort that we must do to achieve the goal. Writing your goals make it much easier to manage the process and to know exactly where we are. It also allows us to check each other to make sure we are on track and allows us to push each other up!

Have you ever been in a place where you did not understand why someone was telling you all of their business? Have you ever been that person who wishes someone had let you know in advance that something was coming up, or wished someone kept you in the loop on something that was important? Have you ever been that person who was told to stop asking so many questions? For years, I did not understand why it was necessary to let others know exactly what I was doing, nor did I pay too much attention to what everyone else was doing, except for when something was not done. For years, I was criticized for asking too many questions that is until I met and began working for Ms. Yarbrough. She has taught me that it is important to communicate what you know when you know it. She encourages others to ask as many questions as needed to get clarity, as long as they are relevant questions. When you over-communicate the need for asking excessive questions lessens. When you over-communicate, no one is left in the dark. You do not have to waste time repeating yourself like a broken record. Over-communicating gives you the responsibility for the clarity of the message. When you over-communicate you get your needs met, and you reduce the opportunity for gaps.

When I started to implement the things, Ms. Yarbrough has coached me on, I saw immediate growth in myself. She has inspired me to stop worrying over making simple decisions. It used to take me sometimes, days, to make a decision because I was always worried about what others might think, or how it might affect others. I would sleep on it, worry about it, and for me, making decisions was never a comfortable thing to do. After a few weeks, and informal lessons from Ms. Yarbrough, I had built more confidence and I found myself making decisions. She let me know that if I did not like the decision I made, or if I decided I could have made a better decision, that I still could and that I should just simply make another decision. It was okay to do that! She told me to "get over myself." It was that easy! I do not know why it took me nearly 35 years to figure that out, but somehow after she explained it, I got it!

Some people say that you have to hit rock bottom before you truly are able to make a decision to change or that the grass is not greener on the other side. I am here to argue and let you know that it is never too early or too late to make a change. Sometimes, the grass really is greener on the other side, but you will never find out unless you believe that it is! Ms. Yarbrough's BAD book is proof that you can choose to begin again differently, at any time regardless of your situation. You need to be able to look at yourself, reflect on your life, and your happenings, and find the motivation you need to do it again differently. Sometimes, it is the little things you change, that make all of the difference in your life. Change will not happen overnight, but if you follow the process, you will see a difference. I certainly have. I am no longer working two full time jobs, I have a renewed passion for what I am doing in all areas of my life, and I am in better control of my finances. I have even developed a strong liking for sweet tea! I am continuing to make progress toward becoming debt-free, all while planning my wedding. I did not know it then, but after reflecting on my life's path, I realized that when I decided to give up control, when I decided to stop making excuses and when I decided to allow God to guide me, I began to appreciate the little things that make life enjoyable. I began to live again with purpose. When I found Ms. Yarbrough, and began self-directing myself under her leadership, I found myself! I did not know it then but finding her was a turning point in my life.

It is my hope that as you read this book, you consider the activities that are provided, and that you take a closer look at yourself. I hope that this book will do for you, what it has been able to do for me. Congratulations on the first step which is choosing to read this book!

Best wishes,

Ashley Radder
Yes Inc. Team Member

INTRODUCTION

"Impossible is just an opinion."
—Paulo Coelho

B eginning Again Differently, or being BAD, is possible for
anyone who refuses to give up. Reading this book, or any
book, means that you believe, too, that anything is possible,
that you can do something differently to get different results. My
hope for each reader is that something is different for you when
you finish this book.

Throughout this book, I reference the many people who I
have "copied" from to become the person that was able to begin
again differently.

As a teacher, for most of my life, I learned early on that we, as educators, steal from each other. If one teacher has a great way to teach the parts of speech, then all others could take the idea or use the plan the same way to get the right results. The same would happen if one teacher had a great lesson planning strategy or a great way to manage student outbursts, then everyone would steal the idea or use the plan to manage their student outbursts. Harry Wong, best-selling author of *The First Days of School,* made the term famous "teachers can steal" by publicly stating that "it is okay for educators to steal" good ideas, strategies that work, practical assignments, and other things teachers do that other teachers don't have to re-create because someone has already done something successfully.

Please don't be surprised when you read this book and see that I reference and give credit to those people who I have learned from to begin again differently. I really believe in not re-creating the wheel a reference to not building another mousetrap. I get great joy in sharing and name-dropping those people who have made a difference in my life.

My disclaimer right away is that people who are powerful and famous are sometimes polarizing, such that people have decided to either hate them or love them. My hope is that you will look towards the messages I share from these people instead of whether you like these people.

I focus a lot in this book about what I've learned from two major influences on my journey of beginning again differently. These people strongly influenced me, and I believe God sent them to help me begin again differently: Dave Ramsey, founder of the Lampco Group, Ramsey Solutions, and bestselling author;

and Joel Osteen, Pastor of Lakewood Church—the largest congregational church in America with 90,000 members—and best-selling author.

I agree that no man is an island, and I believe we all need someone to help us on our journeys in life. By reading and listening to both Dave and Joel, I was able to begin again differently—beginning with listening to hundreds of Joel Osteen's messages on SiriusXM radio every morning starting around 4:30 a.m., and attending my first Entreleadership One-Day Event on October 16, 2016, by listening to Dave explain the concepts in his book, *Entreleadership*.

According to Rockefeller to be successful you need to focus, focus, focus. I encourage you to focus as you read the messages within the seven smart processes so that you can make a decision to begin again differently after suffering a loss.

Chapter 1:

IS THIS YOU?

*"When sorrows come, they come not single spies
but in battalions."*
—William Shakespeare

O kay! It has happened! Your big contract—the one that brought in most of your funding to pay you and your staff, your primary funding source, your business—is gone. You lost it, you gave it away, or you believe someone took or stole it from you. No matter how it happened, it is over.

You may have seen the loss coming. You may have been preparing for the loss of your funding for some time. You may have been surprised, even blindsided, by the loss. No matter how it happened—whether over a year, two, or with one week's or a day's notice—you now know what it feels like to lose something important.

Were you responsible for staff members' livelihoods, and now you have to tell them they do not have a job anymore due to the loss of your major contract or funding? Are you concerned about your reputation in the community as you cease providing services or no longer are seen as an asset to the community?

Are you wondering what will happen next? Are you wondering if it can get any worse? Are you ready to give up on your dream? Or the dream you had when you started your business, your non-profit, your vision? Do you feel like you have nowhere to turn?

Are you thinking about getting a "regular job" now that your dream has ended? Do you want to get a regular job? Can you face getting back into the workforce, interviewing for positions you know are not a good fit for you? Do you think there aren't any good options for your future? Do you feel like you've failed irrevocably, and that there's little hope for moving on positively?

Do any of these questions sound familiar to you regarding the situation you are in, or may be in sooner than you think?

I want you to answer these questions honestly and truthfully *(because I would never tell you to ignore your thoughts about your situation and your perceptions about what is happening to you)*. I want to be clear, though, there really is hope for a brighter future to imagine for yourself—if you are willing to begin again differently, or be BAD, and not give up all hope.

Your loss may have been significant like mine, when I lost a contract we had for eighteen years, and you may feel utterly hopeless, like I did when I realized I would have to tell eighty-three people to find other employment opportunities.

However, like I am sharing with you, there is definitely—dare I say there is guaranteed —hope and brightness waiting for you if you decide that you will not succumb to whatever life has thrown your way that has caused your loss to happen.

There are possibilities that you can experience if you are willing to go on a journey to begin again differently. I have been blessed throughout my life to be conscious of people who proclaim that you can get something for nothing. This book is not about pie-in-the-sky happiness. This book is about the realness of the changes that can happen when you open yourself up to believing and hoping for a better tomorrow. Even if you have to begin believing about hope for hope's sake, the mere act of believing again can do wonders for you as you embrace the possibilities that can exist if you decide not to give up on your dream.

There are so many stories in our world today about life after death, success after failure, and hope after despair, but you may be thinking that your loss cannot have a 'happily ever after' while you're going through it. In fact, it seems like our world has us thinking that we've lost something, that we're the only ones missing something, or we're made to feel that no one has suffered as badly. You may be thinking that what has happened to you is so bad, so ugly, and so unfair that nothing good can possibly come from your loss. I am here to tell you that you are wrong. If you can muster up enough strength to read through this book, with just a glimmer of willingness to read the words on the pages that follow, I believe that you will find the ability to want to begin again differently.

One story that has half of a happy ending involves my friend, Irma. She and her husband ran the biggest daycare in a border town for almost fifteen years. They had several other profitable businesses, as well. Their weekly revenue was between $50,000 and $60,000. They had what looked like a successful business. However, in the matter of several weeks, after a painful IRS audit found that they had not paid some taxes, the business began a downward spiral. It did not help that at the same time the IRS completed their audit and decided what the company owed the government, the economy dried up the jobs in their area so that people who brought children to the daycare stopped coming because they no longer had jobs to pay for it.

The other businesses suffered as well, and within a year, Irma and her husband lost everything. Then, the stress of it all caused Irma's husband to suffer a stress-related heart attack and die. Irma had lost her second husband. As a single mother, she moved to a big city and re-married a wonderful man who died from old age but did not leave her any of his money due to leaving everything to his son from his first marriage.

To be honest, for a while, Irma lost it. She suffered a mild breakdown and was hospitalized for a while. She retired from her job to have funds from her pension to live on. Her youngest daughter, with a young child of her own, began to help her regain her hope again by providing her with her basic needs so that she could begin to function again. At that time, Irma decided not to give up, but to begin again. She went back to work and began saving her retirement pension and living off of her wages. She got her "hope" back and decided not to succumb to the hurt and pain she felt due to her losses.

Today, after ten years, Irma has over a quarter of a million dollars in her bank account. She eventually paid off all of the IRS obligations she incurred from the bankruptcy event that killed her husband, and she is now paying for her grandchildren's college education and is preparing her legacy to live on long after she's gone. Now in her early seventies, Irma is still active, vibrant, and working because she wants to. I share Irma's story because she decided to begin again, even though it was hard after the death of her third husband, suffering a minor breakdown, and having to depend on her youngest daughter for assistance.

Irma is no better than anyone else who has lost and restarted, but she did do something those who give up don't typically do; she decided she would start over or begin again. In Irma's case, she suffered several losses: the loss of her business, which led to the loss of her second husband, which led to her moving to a bigger city and marrying again, and then losing her husband, the house, and her sanity for a while. But now, she believes that it is never too late to begin again, which is exactly what she has been doing for ten years. Is she perfect now? No. But she definitely loves life again with her focus on the seven processes detailed in this book.

It is sometimes easier at the time of your loss—or, in Irma's case, losses—to want to give up. Sometimes you feel like the forces that are coming against you, causing you to lose are making you give up. However, you still have choices you can make. Even if you don't think you have choices, you do. Even if you have no more money, you still have choices you can make. Even if you lost everything through bankruptcy, you still have choices you can make. Even if you lost your home, or worse, even if you lost your family or your loved ones because of the loss of your funding or your business, you still have choices you can make.

Sometimes it will definitely feel like you do not have choices. But this is not true. You always have choices that you can make. All of your options may seem bleak; however, to have a choice of which bleak option to follow means you still have a choice to make.

I believe that, no matter what, if you can find it somewhere within you to decide not to give in or to give up, you will win. Win your joy back, your happiness back, maybe even your job or business back, but definitely your life back to where you can be better in control of your future and your destiny because you decided not to give up and you made a choice to begin again.

I am not saying that anything in this book is easy to do. I am saying that you will definitely decide that what is in this book is worth it to do as you begin to realize that you can begin again. Anyone can begin again, even you—especially you, because you were brave enough to pick up this book and begin reading it.

What will happen to you if you do not finish this book or if you decide that you do not want to begin again? One thing that will definitely happen to you if you decide to succumb to the lost contract, the lost employees, the lost business, or any loss is that you will never know what could have been different for you if you had just tried a do-over. Will you die? Probably not, but something in you may die. Your hope that you had when you started your nonprofit business, or when you got the big contract, or when you hired your team—that may die within you.

What about regrets? I personally try hard not to have regrets, and I do this by being deliberate about the decisions I make that I have to live with. If you make a decision, whether you finish my book or not, not to begin again, what regrets will you have?

By now, everyone—and by everyone, I mean probably billions of people—have heard about the big comeback Tiger Woods had at the recent Master's Golf Tournament, which he won after not winning big for almost eight years. When I read the headlines about Tiger, I thought about all of the failures and losses he had gone through. In most cases, all of Tiger's losses had been by his own doing. He lost his family due to his infidelity. This major loss appeared to hurt his golf game as he stopped winning tournaments. He lost many endorsements from several big companies, and he lost his health.

It was interesting for me to read about his back problems. It appears that the year before he won the 2019 Master's, he had a third back surgery that he thought, along with many sports authorities, would end his career. There are some video clips of famous sports writers and anchors proclaiming that Tiger Woods' best days were gone and that he would never win again. These clips were shown over and over again after Tiger won the 2019 Masters as proof of what?

I believe Tiger's come back was due to him deciding not to give up, but to begin again. While he was already a wealthy man, and he was never in danger of losing his wealth, he lost a lot of credibility and his entire career upon which he had built his life. He was declared a has-been. In the life of someone famous, to be declared a has-been is probably one of the worst monikers that one can be tagged with, as it means one's career is over. A lot of the time, people forget how great one was when he or she was legitimately great because he or she is now a has-been. With one win, Tiger changed the course of his legacy, and his career is now back on. Now, Tiger is projected to break more records by winning more tournaments, and he is back in the winner's circle.

Now, I am not suggesting that I am like Tiger. But I do believe Tiger is like all of us who have experienced loss. He had choices to make about giving up or continuing to pursue his dreams. We have the same choices Tiger had.

When I lost my biggest contract ever, about twenty other entities in my industry lost their contracts, too. Yet I am the only entity still standing after the loss. Did they not try to begin again? What did I do differently that they did not do to restart our company so that we were once again striving? Why didn't my nonprofit close or go away like them? While I do not know everything about their businesses or what caused them to close when they lost their contracts, I do know that our company did something different by being willing to begin again differently. One of the reasons I do not know the specifics regarding why the business like mine went away is because it is difficult to talk to others about your loss, especially when you are going through your loss. Let's be real—it is a difficult conversation to have with anyone.

When you realize this, you get to decide how to utilize that change and whether you do or don't want a do-over.

You may or may not have already done a post-mortem on your failure. A post-mortem, I learned through going to a business workshop, is where you look at a project after it's all over and decide what could have been done differently, what could have worked better, or what the results could have been had you changed some aspect of your program. If you have done a post-mortem, then you may be acutely aware of what happened to cause your loss, and you may be already charting a new course for a new business or a do-over of your current business. If you have not yet looked at what caused the failure, it may be important for you to stop once you can be objective and complete a review of what led to your loss.

While I think that it is definitely important at some point in the process of beginning again to know what led to the loss, I don't believe you have to figure out all of the nuances associated with what caused the loss if the information is not readily reviewable by you. Yes, it is important to know what happened as you do not ever want the loss to happen again; however, I am confident that you will want to reflect on some other aspects of beginning again as well.

This is what I now know about failing and losing. We all do it in some ways, hours, days, weeks, months, and years of our lives, and we rarely die from failing and losing. Failure is not fatal, nor is it final. We get to decide how we will deal with succeeding after failing because it is possible to come out on the other side better than you were before. It is a choice that you can make.

This book includes three parts. Part One includes three chapters that focus on examples of losses. Chapter 2 is my personal loss story, and Chapter 3 is an overview of how to begin again after a loss.

Part Two includes the seven chapters on the 7 Smart Process I learned to use after my loss to begin again differently. I believe these smart processes will work for anyone who wants to begin again to win again. At the end of each chapter, there is a BAD: Begin Again Differently thought or activity which will help illustrate some possible next steps in your journey towards winning again.

Part Three includes Chapter 11, with a focus on overcoming any obstacles that you believe may hinder you from continuing your work toward winning after a loss. And Chapter 12 is the obvious conclusion to the book, but not to your story, as you will make a decision to continue working toward a win.

Begin Again Differently (BAD) Thought Chapter #1:

Did you answer the question posed by this chapter? Write down your thoughts as to why this is or is not a description of you.

Chapter 2:
EAT DIRT

*"What's right is what's left
if you do everything else wrong."*
—Robin Williams

One day my twin sister, my younger sister, my mom, and I moved from the basement apartment where I would make dirt pies and eat them as part of one of our kid games to the Cabrini Greens Homes at 706 Division Street, Chicago, Illinois. The Cabrini Greens were a step up in the world for my mom, my sisters, and me. It was a high-rise apartment building, maybe twenty or more floors, and we no longer would be living in the one-room basement apartment where my mom's friend, Penny, had agreed to let us stay while my mom waited for our apartment to be approved. These are some of my earliest memories of life, right before everything changed when we moved into the Cabrini Greens projects.

I knew we were dirt-poor right away, but let me say, for the record, that my mom never had a poverty mindset, nor did she say we were poor. A poverty mindset is where you are not only physically poor without means, resources, and most importantly, money, but you also are mentally poor. This means you "think like you're poor." When you think "poor," you think that there's no hope to ever get means, resources, or money, so you act out like there are no other options in the world for you. Whatever you say, "goes." Whatever you do, "so what." Whatever it is, "is" because there's not a lot of caring when you have a poverty mindset. But I always knew we were poor because we did not have food sometimes; the refrigerator was usually empty.

My mom always had faith in God that she would one day buy a house. The minute we moved into the projects; my mom talked about one day owning her own home. I think that my mom never had a poverty mindset because my mom was raised on a forty-acre farm in Mississippi that her mom and dad owned.

My mom was the oldest of six children, and growing up, she never had to go without food, shelter, or the necessities of life. I can imagine that it was somewhat difficult for her to find herself living in the projects with three girls as a single mom in the state of poverty. On the farm, my mom's family raised hogs and cattle and farmed vegetables. In Chicago, in the projects, we often went without because to get food required money, and we were poor.

I often thought the reason we were poor was that my mother married the wrong man, and then I would think that, if she had not married my father, then I would not have been born, so I would always catch myself to make sure I did not say this thought out loud. The hard truth was in the sixties lots of African American people were poor.

In the late fifties and early sixties, lots of African Americans from the South, especially Mississippi, moved away from the harshness of southern life where racial inequity was the norm in the hopes of finding a better life up North, or in my mom's case, in the Midwest—Chicago, Illinois. My mom graduated from Lane College in Jackson, Mississippi, with a degree in nutrition so that she could work as a dietitian in a hospital. She moved from her home in the South with the hopes of finding a job in Chicago.

As we got older, she would often tell us of the rooming houses where she lived, and while we were growing up, she would often take us on the weekends to revisit parts of Chicago where she was a young woman working before she met dad and they got married. She shared stories of when her sisters would visit her from Mississippi to check on her and make sure she was doing okay. Therefore, so many people from my mom's hometown moved to Chicago around the time she did, my mom had a pretty extensive friend presence in Chicago, and we got to visit with them often and listen to the stories they would tell about their lives in Mississippi before they moved to Chicago.

Cabrini Greens has since become synonymous with some of the failed social policies of the sixties that were supposed to provide affordable housing temporarily for poor people so that they could bootstrap themselves out of abject poverty into the middle class. Instead, projects like Cabrini Green became hotbeds for crimes, delinquencies, and murders. I remember when the first woman to be elected Chicago's mayor, Mayor Jane Byrd, moved into Cabrini Green to make a statement about how safe the projects were and on the night she moved in, someone was murdered, and within three weeks she and her police presence had moved out. The projects did not accomplish what the government intended, but for my family, it sure felt good to have a five-room apartment instead of the one-bedroom basement apartment.

We lived in Cabrini Green from when I was in kindergarten until I was in seventh grade when we moved because my mom purchased a home. Homeownership had always been important to my mom because she grew up on a farm that her parents owned. For seven years, between 1964 and 1971, each summer, my mom would go to the bank to buy a house, and each summer, she would return home and say not this year, maybe next year. One summer, we asked why we weren't getting a house, and she explained that she had to pay off some debt that belonged to my father.

When my father married my mom, it was over the objections of my mom's family. I think they knew something that she refused to see at the time, but she married my dad anyway. In 1964, we lived in the basement apartment before we moved to Cabrini Green because my mom and my dad had finally separated. My mom did not say anything at the time, but now I know, my dad was a rolling stone. This means that my dad had multiple women and multiple families. We met two of my father's other families eventually and found out we had a half-brother and a half-sister. They were much older than my sisters and me, and they were already married with children, so we became aunts to nieces that were just a bit younger than us. My mother was also good friends with my half-brother and half-sister's mother as well. My father's other woman's family was not close to us at all, as her children were from her first husband. But still, our father often brought my sisters and me to this house for weekend visits and other activities.

My father owned a furniture store and would sometimes take us to his furniture store on the weekends. I don't remember many customers, but I do remember for lunch he would buy us huge foot-long hotdogs with plenty of French fries and ketchup. My father was not poor, just my mother. Whenever we were with my father, we ate pretty well.

706 Division Street is now a million-dollar property in Chicago, and there is no evidence in 2019 of the high-rise projects that were once located there.

I started my book with a review of my past and an indication to the reader that I know even if you grow up in poverty as I did, there is obviously hope that you can achieve your dreams depending upon what you want out of life. If someone from the Cabrini Green apartments can dream and achieve, anyone can.

How does a girl go from living in some of the most notorious housing projects in the nation to a three-acre luxury home worth over a half million dollars?

First of all, my mom finally bought the house. In the summer of 1971, we moved from the Cabrini Greens to the Rosalind neighborhood on the South side of Chicago into a two-story, three-bedroom, two-bathroom home with a foyer, a living room, a small den, an eat-in kitchen, a back porch, and a huge pantry and great back yard. My mom was still suffering from some income insecurities because she had become a teacher instead of continuing as a dietitian in order to be on the same work schedule as our school schedules, and she had started as a teacher's aide. Because she and my dad never divorced, she never received child support. While teacher pay is lower than in most professions, it was even lower in the 1970s. We were living from paycheck to paycheck, but we were in a home. I remember being a huge Cubs baseball fan and watching Fergie Jenkins pitch from our television in our den., We always had the best dressers, television stands, and bedroom sets because of my dad's furniture store. People would visit us and be puzzled at our house because everyone knew we were poor, but our furniture told a different story.

I believe everyone has a story to tell, even if it is not a poverty story, because it is important how you were raised and the environment you grew up in; it usually has an impact on what you do in life or what you choose to do with your life. As a side note to my story, Hollywood has often gone through stretches in its history where actors were encouraged to have a rags to riches story, and then sometimes it was a big deal to proclaim that the actor never wanted for anything. Whether or not your story matters to anyone other than your family and friends, it is important to be aware of the way your parents raised you.

While we were growing up in the projects without a poverty mindset, we were also growing in the church with a focus on God, Jesus, prayer, and praise. My mom was one of the most positive people alive, so despite her circumstances—marrying the wrong man, living in Cabrini Greens, making low wages, and being poor—we never really talked about poverty or of being poor.

Believe it or not, I did not know that I grew up in Cabrini Greens until after we moved away in 1971. I was walking down the street of 108th Place near my new home with a friend as she talked about some bad stuff that happened the night before based upon a news story she had heard. I asked her where it had happened, she mentioned the address to Cabrini Greens and I said, "Hey, I think that is where we just moved from." I am not saying I did not know that I had grown up in the projects, I just did not know at the time that the projects where I had grown up had actually been the infamous Cabrini Greens Homes.

I went to kindergarten through sixth grade at Schiller Elementary School right behind the Cabrini Greens, and right away from my enrollment, I knew I loved school. My mom took us every weekend to the library and to the mobile library that came to the Cabrini Green Homes regularly, so I already loved books, but school was my haven. When the blizzard of 1963 hit Chicago and there were mountains of over-packed snow everywhere, I went to school by climbing over the snow-packed mountains that formed on the blacktop between Cabrini Greens and the school. I am not sure if schools had snow days in the 60s, but my teacher was there with my favorite pretzel snack and donuts, and we had school. I've always wanted to be a teacher ever since I can remember because I only have positive thoughts about school and learning.

I graduated from Chicago State University, formally the Chicago State Teachers' College, with an English degree, ready to teach. However, there were no teaching jobs to be had in Chicago, so I applied everywhere else, depending upon what school districts came to our college's career fair, and eventually, I was hired to teach in Austin, Texas. In 1981, I moved. I moved again to San Antonio, Texas in 1985 when I married and settled down to continue teaching. However, something was happening in San Antonio regarding poor people.

I got a job teaching in Edgewood Independent School District (EISD). EISD was the poorest school district in Texas at the time, and our superintendent, Mr. Vasquez, had just become famous for suing the Texas Education Agency over the way schools were funded. From 1995 until 2019, this issue is still being legislated with many, many court rulings along the way. Mr. Jerry Vasquez won several awards that year, as well as Superintendent of the Year for his bravery and courage to sue the state on behalf of the children.

After my time teaching in EISD and watching the actions of Mr. Vasquez, something happened to me that changed me from just wanting to teach. You see, I had never, ever been accused of being ambitious, since all I ever wanted to be was a teacher. Most people jeered at me because wanting to become a teacher was not seen as a worthy profession when you were young and a college graduate. And now, working in the poorest district in the state had me thinking differently. I applied for and was accepted into the prestigious Breckenridge Fellowship Program at Trinity University so that I could get a free master's degree in Urban Studies. I wanted to learn more about our local government and gain insight on why our superintendent was suing the State of Texas. I found it was due to the many inequities of poor communities and their education, as well as other services like streets, sidewalks, and neighborhood.

At the same time, Mr. Vasquez was making headlines, another city leader was becoming prominent. Henry Cisneros became a popular mayor and national political figure. Everyone was amazed at how powerful Henry was becoming because, in the city of San Antonio's charter, the mayor only gets one vote, just like the other ten councilmen who made up our city government. So why, then, was Mayor Cisneros getting everything he wanted and seemed to have everyone on his side with only the ability to cast one vote like everyone else? Lots of people who graduated from the fellowship program at Trinity University went on to work for the City of San Antonio as city managers and department heads. I thought maybe getting my master's degree in Urban Studies would be a way I could get into city government to help poverty-stricken areas like Edgewood ISD. As a teacher in Edgewood ISD, I felt drawn to the plight of the people living in poverty because of my life growing up in Cabrini Greens.

Next Part of the Story

I heard about the charter school movement after I had started two different free schools for high school students who were being legally targeted by their school districts to drop out of the educational system due to delinquent behavior and, in some cases, generational delinquent behavior because an older brother or sister had been a menace to the traditional schools. I helped, on a small scale, individual students—about five in total—to earn their high school diplomas.

Our nonprofit, Youth Empowerment Services, Inc., which I founded in 1995, had also been recognized for running a two-month summer program where 500 students from sixteen different districts in San Antonio, Texas, worked together side-by-side without one fight or altercation between students. After the Texas Department of Commerce (TDOC in 1995) visited our site and proclaimed our program 'exemplary, I began thinking that, if we could start a charter school, we could have access to students year-round. If the impact we had in just six weeks were an indication of our prowess for helping educate youngsters toward successful educational achievements and healthy relationships without fighting, we would be on to something.

In 1998, the state approved our charter application to create the Higgs, Carter, King Gifted and Talented Charter Academy. It was rated sixth out of eighty-two charter applications. We opened September 1, 1998. Right away, we experienced severe organizational problems. At the time, I kept comparing ourselves to David Robinson, former NBA San Antonio Spurs Basketball Star and future Hall of Famer who had started his own school after five years of discussions, planning, preparing and researching best practices on how to start a school. I remember saying and thinking this thought often when we were struggling, "I wish we had had five years to start our school." Maybe then we would not have the issues we had with our Charter.

Many of the issues, in hindsight, had to do with my leadership. I had the absolute right heart to do what was needed and what I thought was necessary; however, I did not operate effectively in how to actually get everyone on the same page. We had tons of communication issues and problems with parents and staff. One staff member told parents we had a technology program. When a parent called me to complain about us not having a technology program, I confirmed that a technology program was written into our proposal to open the charter school, but the state did not give us funding for a technology program, therefore, we did not have a technology program.

After heated conversations throughout that first year with lots of staff and parents about the misunderstandings and unclear communication, we started our second year with just six teachers from the first year, when we had had over twenty-five, and just under 200 students when we had initially opened with almost 400 and another 400 on the waiting list. We slowly got better and better at communicating with teachers, parents, staff, and students, and we began to grow in enrollment as we focused on getting better at running our charter school as a nonprofit.

Fast forward to 2013. We had developed a great relationship with the community, our enrollment was between 600 and 750 students annually (including 250 three and four-year-old pre-kinder students), and we had employed eighty-three full-time staff. We were rocking our ability to communicate more effectively with everyone. We had 1,200 parents and students regularly attend and participate in all of our mandatory parent involvement activities. We always offered free food while parents worked alongside their children, learning more ways to help their children improve academically. I believed I was living more than my dream because all I ever wanted to be was a teacher, and now I was a charter school superintendent and principal as well as the chief executive officer of our nonprofit. I was often telling myself that I was on cloud nine, a reference to being high-as-a-kite on life without any influences.

What I did not realize at the time was that I was sinking. I regularly worked twelve to sixteen-hour days, and I believed that my lifestyle was healthy. I left work after midnight most nights, Monday through Sunday, and arrived back at work no later than 6:30 AM. I went through all of the motions, and I thought I was leading well. Most people called me brilliant behind my back and to my face, but I realized that something was not right. I could not put my finger on it. Then, I heard rumors that the state legislature, in its attempt to take control of the charter school industry, introduced a bill to close charter schools based upon a series of factors that were retroactive to three years before 2013. Everyone I talked to assured me that the bill would never pass, but pass it did, and later on that year, we found out that our charter school was on the list to be closed.

I was horrified. But I was a positive person by nature, so I rested assured and prayed believing that the list was wrong, and the information was incorrect. I thought at the time that all I had to do was keep the faith, and I was sure God would work out this issue with the new law in our favor. I organized our parents, students, and staff and we went to the state capitol on several occasions and testified about our school that was, at the time, rated the highest level you could rate for student progress. Our students, parents, and staff talked about their love for the school, its long eighteen-year history, and the good it did over the years.

We hired a consultant who met with the commissioner and other people at the state level to champion our desire to save our school. Our consultant regularly shared with me that when she spoke to the people, she met with, they all assured her that our school had never been the target of the new law, but somehow we were caught up in the new law, Senate Bill 2 due to the retro-activeness included in the bill.

We finally had to break the news to our parents that even though we would continue to fight, we would not be a charter school in the upcoming school year. A lot of our parents accepted this information and made other decisions to enroll their children in other charter schools. However, 250 of our parents refused to go to another school, so our nonprofit board of directors agreed to allow us to utilize over $783,000 to provide tuition-free private school education to the parents for one year while we continued to fight for our school in court.

It soon became evident that without funding, the $783,000 covered basically the teachers and the other staff members. We owned all of the property already, but we could not provide transportation services to ninety percent of the students who required bus services. The 250 students by the end of the year became less than 125, and we officially stopped the tuition-free private school education after one year. Later that year, the Texas Supreme Court ruled that the state had the right to close the schools, including ours, so we officially closed our doors.

On June 30, 2015, we officially lost our primary funding source of eighteen years—four million dollars.

I pondered how could this have happened after all of the hard work of everyone involved, after a long positive history of serving the community, after being recognized for countless accomplishments and milestones. Why was our charter school going away?

I laid in bed one afternoon, curled up in a fetal position, shortly after the realization numbness had worn off, crying, again. After a while, I heard a very still, small voice speak to me.

I initially ignored the voice as I cried, "It was not fair!"—"and what about the eighty-three staff members who had not done anything wrong. Why are they losing their jobs?"

"They had depended upon me specifically because I was the leader," I cried.

Then I began listening to the small voice in my spirit—that I believe was God, and I heard something so clearly that "the eighty-three people were never your responsibility anyway."

I said, "What?"

Then I believe I heard God (somewhere in my spirit) explain very clearly to me that I had been acting like I was in charge for eighteen years when in reality it had been HIM in charge all along. As I was lying there thinking through what I believe God was telling me, I began to realize that I had probably stopped listening to his guidance consistently over the past 18 years. I also began thinking that I had been going through the motions of working and leading, but that I had not been leading exactly like God would have had me lead because I had stopped consistently allowing him to guide me.

Remember me mentioning several pages ago the law that was passed retroactively? God reminded me that afternoon that He had given me several opportunities to close out our high school program, but I never listened. I always made some excuse that we were really helping these troubled youth. As I began thinking some more about this revelation, I realized that in reality, we were not helping them. They had been causing distractions and taken a lot of time and energy away from the other students with their inappropriate language and actions that we had never been able to tame. Over ninety-five percent of the students were in pre-kindergarten to eighth grade, and only less than five percent were high school students, but they had taken up all of our time every year with behavior issues, court issues, disrespect issues and much, much, more.

That afternoon, God took me through a journey over the past several years where He showed me several times when He had tried to get my attention to do things differently, but I made decisions opposite of what He had been trying to get me to do. I stopped crying and began reflecting on what I believed God was showing me. God finally shared that because the eighty-three employees had never been my responsibility anyway and that He had always been in charge even though I had not always let Him lead. I believe I heard God say, "I've got this. I've got those eighty-three employees. You don't have to cry over them. They were never your responsibility; they've always been My responsibility. Got it?"

I said, "Yes and thank you, Lord," and I went through the most restful sleep I had in almost eighteen months since beginning the fight to save our school.

The next morning, I woke up, jumped out of bed, and stood still. I was giddy, laughing and waiting with excitement to see what God was about to do for me now that I had decided to stop trying to be in charge. I said to God, "Okay, God, I'm putting You back in charge of everything. No more Claudette being in the way of Your wishes and desires for what I am on this earth to do. Lead the way." I jumped up and down for joy—a weight lifted off of me. I realized that as long as I put God first in everything, *now* whatever happened would be what God wanted to happen and that I was no longer in charge. I stopped, and said, "Okay God what do You have for me to do today?" When I got to work that day, I met with our remaining team members. Over the next several days, weeks, and months, I shared my story of failing to allow God to lead, but now I was ready to follow God's lead for our agency and that I was changing, and the agency would need to change as well.

It was a slow process, but I began to take one day at a time by remembering through the day to put God first in everything, no matter how big or small.

Here's what I knew for sure:

- God's got this! I would be ready to accept His will for our agency.
- God gave us the nonprofit, and no matter what happened, no one could take our legacy away. Just because the state decided to take our contract, did not mean our history nor our legacy would go away. We would always have our accomplishments to cherish, all of the lives of parents and students we changed, all of the letters, commendations, and recommendations we had received after serving the community for eighteen years, and everything good about us, would not go away just because we lost our funding.
- God had something different He wanted us to do. I had always hesitated in the past to say things like "God's got something better for you," or when someone's divorcing or losing a spouse, "God's got someone better for you."

I always wanted to say that God's got something different for you. Only time could tell whether the "different" thing would be better for you.

I don't believe my refusal to say or think "God's got something better for me" is showing a lack of faith. It's not that I did not have that kind of faith, but rather that the word *better* could be subjected to whatever anyone thought was better. Since I did not know at this point what God had in store for our agency, I did not feel comfortable saying God's got something better. I felt comfortable saying, "God's will, will be done, whatever it is."

When we lost our major annual contract of over $4 million, we still had one other Educator Effectiveness contract that was extended for one final year, and so we steadfastly continued the work we had to accomplish on that contract. Then, in May 2016, we received word that there would be a competition for one final installment of the Educator Effectiveness contract. It would be due in July 2016, and we would know if we won the competition on October 1, 2016. Our team worked and submitted our plan for the Educator Effectiveness contract in July 2016. On October 1, 2016, I received an email that our project was accepted along with fourteen others out of 800 proposals for funding.

Our new five-year contract that began October 2016 was for $54 million. This was the largest contract we had ever been awarded, and I knew without a doubt that putting God first in the way I was leading was instrumental in the way we wrote the project that was funded. The next year, we were awarded another five-year contract for almost $10 million. Our annual budget is now nearly three times the $4 million we lost, and the future is looking bright because of the way we are continuously focusing on doing things differently versus how we were doing them when I lost the contract.

What I intentionally began to do differently that caused me to change how I was leading was to not lead like I was a 'lone ranger... making all decisions without collaborating or even seeking guidance from God'. Now what is different is that I consistently and constantly seek guidance from my heavenly father, and this has lead me to be a leader that is able to collaborative meaningfully with my teammates in leading our company.

This is what I know now about the failure I experienced when I lost our contract: my failure was not the end of my story, and the failure you may have experienced or are experiencing as you face a loss does not have to be the end of your dream.

I am continuing to learn that to begin again differently is a process and not a one-time event. This process is becoming more and more useful as a daily process that is helping me to change the trajectory of our agency. We are continuing to get on track to be where we believe we can now grow and expand.

Avoid Regrets

I have thought long and hard about not having regrets since I was a teenager. I would look in the mirror after a hard conversation had gone wrong, or I had not stood up for myself after being told something negative about a friend. I would try to recreate the incident to see what I would have said or done differently.

I grew tired of always thinking to myself, "you should have said...this" or "you should have done...this" to have enjoyed a different consequence after an incident.

Later in life, I learned that people "should" not "should" on other people. I began to utilize a different kind of mindset by saying people "should also not should on themselves." "Shoulding on people or shoulding" on yourself is a great way to have regrets. I have learned over the years to not "should" on myself or others, and I believe I have been more at peace with myself because I avoid and deliberately ensure that I don't think thoughts like what I should or should not have done.

What I have learned to do instead is to focus on what I can do differently next time a similar conversation or incident occurs. This may sound simple and too easy of a thing to do when beginning again differently! It is. And it works! It works because you will begin to focus on what you need to change rather than regretting a previous incident where you may have said or done something you plan to do differently next. The important thing to remember is to focus on what to do next time that will be different rather than regretting the mistake you just made.

Really focusing on getting better *next time* gives you a feeling of knowing that you will get an opportunity for a *do-over.* I now love knowing that even if I had really missed a golden opportunity to do something differently, getting a "next time" was a comforting thought because I knew I was going to be more effective in the next conversation or the next incident with different results. One of the reasons why having regrets makes no sense is that you will likely have a similar opportunity later in life to do something different. Spending a lot of time regretting your actions is not the best way to begin doing things differently. I am not saying anything about being remorseful for something wrong you've done. I am saying that spending a lot of time talking and thinking regretful thoughts will hinder your ability to begin to change.

Another reason having regrets is senseless is that you cannot "turn back the hands of time" (a reference to a Smokey Robinson song). No one can go back in time and correct a failed conversation or a terrible incident. Because it is not possible to go back in time, why regret what has already happened? Why not take the time to focus on being ready to handle a similar conversation or incident differently next time as opposed to worrying about what has happened in the past.

I have tried very hard to live my life going forward without regretting decisions I have made or things I have done. Even if I have majorly messed up (i.e., losing the contract would be a major mess up), I never had lingering regrets. Don't get me wrong, I may be saddened, I definitely cried, I was upset, and I thought it was unfair. I did not like what happened to me, to my company, and to our employees. However, during the time of one of my greatest most public loss, I never regretted what happened to me as I resolved to do things differently next time.

I am not saying that it was easy. In fact, I am saying just the opposite. It was tough to suffer the loss of my company's most significant contract at the time. However, I deliberately resolved to not succumb to should have and shouldn't have thoughts. I made it a point to think about what to do differently next time.

In fact, after I woke up that morning mentioned earlier with the knowledge that God was in control, and all I needed to do was follow, I began to be thankful for my failure. Please, please, please keep reading. I know this is a hard pill to swallow, but my gratefulness for my failure is what I believe led me on the path that my company is on now, toward growth and expansion.

The first time I shared that I do not regret my failure and that I was, in fact, grateful for my failures was so freeing. Everyone stared at me as I was in the middle of my presentation to forty school leaders. We talked about the power of reflection, and I shared a little bit of my story. The room got strangely quiet after my announcement that my failure was actually a great thing for my company. I explained, further, that I would never wish for the kind of heartbreak that happened when I failed on my worst enemy. However, I very firmly and clearly said that I did not regret my failure, and in fact, I was learning that my failure was a great thing to happen to me. This was late March 2016, and I did not know at the time that we would be submitting a plan in July 2016, and I certainly did not know at the time that we would be awarded our company's largest contract later that year in October 2016. As I was sharing about my failure to the leaders, I began to experience the same freedom again when I woke up that morning months earlier, realizing that putting God first in everything was what God wanted me to do all along.

I knew that I did not know what our future held. But I also knew that God was going to do something different and no matter what it was, it was going to help us begin again differently.

Are you ready to learn to implement the Seven Smart Processes to begin again differently? Read the next chapters and finish the book, and then let's talk some more about helping you to move forward on your quest to relive or restart your dream to begin winning again.

Recently, my brother-in-law asked me to tell him the details of what happened when we lost our primary funding. At the time, I was in the middle of writing this book and did not want to go into the gory details. When I told him I would talk to him later, I realized that it was still painful, even though our company is on the other side of our loss to talk about. We are thriving again, but it still hurt to talk about it. Even now, every time I tell my story of our loss, it pains me a little. I did not like losing what I worked hard for after eighteen years. I cried a lot during the time immediately following my loss. I had some hard moments with myself as I realized the magnitude of our loss and what it meant and what it would mean if we did not begin again. I stopped eating because my appetite went away for a while. However, I say this with all honesty, and I have said it to many people in workshops and speaking engagements, I do not regret my loss, and I would not wish anything differently to have happened to me. I realized soon after I began again that one of the greatest events of my life had been the major loss of my eighteen-year contract because, through the loss, I became a better leader, a better mother, a better employer, a better Christian, a better friend, and a better person.

I now know that through the eighteen years of having the big contract, I was just going through the motions. What I became aware of was the acronym "TTWWADI: That's The Way We've Always Done It" pronounced, "ttawadi." One of the examples of this is the commercial where the Dunkin Donut cook is making the donuts in his sleep because that's the way he's always done it or *TTWWADI*. When we act like this in business, it is usually because we are part of a bureaucracy where form after form has to be completed before anything gets done, and then most likely it will have to re-done because there was no one really caring what was happening, they were just going through the motions. Now, if you had asked me during any part of the eighteen years, I was running my business, I would have argued and disagreed that I was not doing a TTWWADI. However, as I looked back on my life after the eighteen-year contract loss, I saw many instances of how I was just trying to survive in the business by doing whatever was required to stay in business, but I was not growing or changing or becoming better. I just was. This was hard to admit because during the eighteen years I ran the non-profit, our business had many accomplishments and successes and helped lots of people; however, I could see after my loss how much more we could have done had I been doing things differently. My loss led me to look at my world differently through different lenses because when you suffer a significant loss, whether you like it or not, it changes you.

Smart Process Idea from a Company Team Member:

I started working at the company six months ago. I had done some contract work with the company for about a year before I moved and took on a full-time position with the company.

I began immediately thinking that I had died and gone to heaven because I was so happy to be finally doing work that mattered and that was extremely enjoyable. I also began thinking that I had wasted my life for the past seventy-seven years living in another city when I could have been working here at the company in Texas. The CEO checked me every time I would begin lamenting that it took me seventy-seven years to find my true calling in life. She would say things like, "Stop saying you regret the former years of your life, God had a reason for allowing you to live where you were until now." Or she would say something like, "Stop dissing your former city, you lived there for a reason and now God has you living here for a reason."

She also encouraged me to take one day at a time on this journey with the company, and she insisted that I not compare my former life to my new wonderful life now.

She often reminds me that there is a reason that at seventy-seven years old I am often compared to a much younger man of around forty due to my good health, my great energy and the way I can do things that much younger men struggle to do.

She always encourages me to live in the moments without having regrets. I hope to live another seventy-seven year, enjoying my new-found way of looking and loving my life.

Begin Again Differently (BAD) Thought Chapter #2:

Don't be afraid to think about your losses and write down your thoughts. This will help you start to confront some of what may be hindering you from thinking you can win again. At the very least, it will force you to think, even a little bit, more objectively about the loss you have suffered and maybe allow you to stop regretting things that have happened as you look to your ability to begin again differently.

Chapter 3:

BEGIN AGAIN DIFFERENTLY

"Learn from yesterday, live for today,
hope for tomorrow."
—Albert Einstein

B eginning again differently requires the willingness to be okay with doing something different. The reason I named this book "Begin Again Differently" and not "Begin Again Being Better" is because I wanted to emphasize that doing things differently may or may not be better than actions you took before you experienced your loss. Whether different or better, what you will get are different results, even if all you do is change one thing that will be better for your company.

Focus on Failure When Doing Things Differently

I know that there are different thoughts about failure because to say failure or to believe in failure would appear to be something that is the opposite of what you would want to do. Shouldn't you focus on success if you're going to be successful? My thoughts are that you don't have to limit yourself to concentrate on just one thing, as I don't believe a focus on failure means that you aren't also focusing on success.

My first significant realization of the power of focusing on failure came from Dr. Kathryn Parker Boudett, a Harvard Professor and author of the book series on being data wise. During a conference where Dr. Boudett spoke, she ended her speech by passing out one blank index card, and she said, "Please write a plus (+) symbol on the side of the card. Then write a delta symbol (triangle) on the other side of the card."

She continued by saying, "Now please write down what you think went well during my talk on data on the plus side of the card. When you finish, turn the card over and write what you think could have been more effective on the side of the card with the delta symbol."

As I followed her instructions, the next words she uttered almost made me fall out of my chair. She said, "I learn much more from my deltas than from my pluses. So please be free to tell me your real thoughts about what I could have done differently that may have made our time together today more effective."

Really, I asked myself silently, "I can learn more from my failure than my successes?"

At that time, I had been made aware of the concept that "failure leads to success" from Debbie Deporter and her work on the

Quantum camps and Quantum learning, where "failure leads to success" is described as one of the eight keys of excellence. However, I had never heard anyone say that we learn more from our failure than our success, much less someone who is a Harvard professor. I was amazed. Everyone left the room, and I stayed seated, thinking about the earth-shattering news I just learned from a Harvard professor. We learn more from our failures than our successes. Wow! This perspective from Dr. Boudett gave me ammunition to use, even though I did not know just how powerful this information would be for me going forward, I knew going forward, that I was going to begin to focus on failure differently.

Delta Forces

Please accept that the use of the word "failure" is not a bad word and explaining your loss as a failure is not a bad thing to do. The focus I am suggesting is not the focus on telling yourself things like:

- You're a failure
- You stink
- You lost the contract
- Everyone knows you're stupid
- You believe you're stupid
- How could you do something so stupid
- No one will trust you again
- Any other self-deprecating thoughts that can creep into your mind from others speaking to you and about you or you speaking about you.

There is no benefit to calling yourself names or allowing anyone else to call you names. First off, I have never, ever been this kind of person or said these kinds of things about myself or anyone else for that matter. However, I've heard people talk to themselves this way.

If you are the kind of person who has done and said these kinds of things about you in the past, you will immediately want to stop at this point in your life and promise yourself that you will never think or say things like this about you ever again. Please begin to change your thinking, especially your negative thoughts about yourself. I am trusting that you will immediately make a commitment to never repeating these kinds of things ever about any mistake or failure you have going forward. Words and thoughts are powerful, and when you change the way you're thinking, you can absolutely change your future.

Then, if I am not saying beat yourself up with your thoughts about failure, what do I mean when I say focus on the failure?

The former president of Xerox and first female president of a Fortune 500 company made a comment when she took over the fledgling company years ago.

"When the cow falls in the ditch, we do not need to form a committee to discuss anything about the cow. First, we need to get the cow out of the ditch, then we can analyze what happened and how the cow got in the ditch… so it doesn't happen again."

She was really saying put the *most important things* first. We have to focus on what happened first, do things that immediately address the failure, and then we need to analyze the failure to see that it does not occur again. This quote amplifies that failures will happen, but that's not the most important thing. The most important thing is to recognize the failure for what it is, and then go about focusing on what needs to change.

In our current society, and especially at this time in our country's history, we shy away from acknowledging failure because to accept failure in some ways means that you are accepting your defeat. I believe this could not be further from the truth. The general thought about failure is that failure is bad, and you don't want to give thoughts to bad things, you want to give thoughts to the good and stay positive.

I am strongly suggesting that a focus on failure is a way of being positive. You can positively predict that when you focus on failure, things change for the better. Just to be clear, I am quite aware that what I am suggesting will not sit well with everyone, and it may take you some time to grasp the power of the concept that failure is good.

One time, a mother withdrew her daughter after one year from our school because of our focus on failure. You see, we said the eight keys of excellence every morning, and her daughter was a first grader, and she just did not believe that her daughter should be saying, failure leads to success. Especially since she was saying, like one of our former presidents, failure is not an option.

I agreed with her that she should take her daughter to a school where they shared their beliefs because we firmly knew from experience that failure leads to success.

What do people mean when they say, "Failure is not an option?" I think they mean that we want to overcome failure and not dwell on it, because they cannot possibly mean that no one will ever fail because we, human beings, fail in something or with someone every day.

If failure is not an option, then what is it? I really believe that most people say 'failure is not an option" as an excellent way of being positive, but I absolutely believe that it is not valid. I believe that failure is absolutely an option, as it happens more often than not. A better use of our time and our words is a focus on our failures so that we change and do things differently rather than saying something is not an option when it is.

Smart Processes

The smart processes in this book work when they are practiced continuously. You cannot hope to experience significant changes in your circumstances if you are unwilling to ensure that you will do things consistently differently than before your loss. The first smart thing you will want to do is to commit to learning to utilize these smart processes always. The smart processes are not new processes as people have been using them for years before our time to be successful. I share the smart processes at this time because I never knew after eighteen years, I would be beginning again differently, and I was really amazed at how well they worked for me. The smart processes were there when I needed them, and they are here for you now because you need them. Jeff Bishop, an online motivator, says that if you want to be in the top one percent of your industry you will not get there doing what the other ninety-nine percent are doing. I want to encourage you as you begin again differently begin doing what the others may not be doing.

Smart Process #1: The necessity of believing again in your dreams, in yourself, and your hope for your future. The process of believing may not seem important when you've lost money, business, friends, families, houses, and other resources. However, in this book, I say that having the power to begin believing again is paramount to gaining back what you have lost.

Smart Process #2: Focus on determining or re-determining your *why*. One of the first things we did differently when we lost our contract was to look at why we should exist. Our company revisited Simon Sinek's golden circle and his explanation of why our "why" is more important than "what we do" and "how we do it." We made the decision to make time with remaining staff to re-do our mission and vision, and to establish core values. I am not proud to say this, but it is true. When we lost our contract I, along with our nonprofit board of directors, realized that, with me leading them, the school had a mission and vision, but now that the school had lost the contract, we realized that the board of directors did not have a mission, vision, or core values for the nonprofit.

I was shocked and surprised that I let us work for eighteen years without having a nonprofit vision and mission. We immediately began the process of working on an agency mission, vision, and some core values, and I believe this is a significant change when you can either establish your first mission, vision, and core values, or revisit and revise what you have to more clearly represent that you are now doing things differently. This chapter takes a look at the importance of having goals and the goal setting processes to ensure that your *why* is realized as you continue to begin again.

Smart Process #3: Focus on the power of using over-communication to ensure that clear communication exists in every situation within your company, your professional life, and with family members. For the eighteen years before we lost our contract, if you would have asked me about my communication skills or asked anyone who was working with me, I am pretty sure I would have gotten high marks.

After the loss of the contract, I viewed communication and the value of clear communication differently. I learned from Dave Ramsey how to promote overcommunication as a great way to make sure you have clear communication with everyone. To begin again differently, you will learn how to become comfortable with overcommunicating so that your company has appropriate transparent conversations as a matter of how you and your team members work together every day.

When you have a high level of transparency in your communication, everything functions better. Your day-to-day work seems to flow even if sometimes the communication is not always positive, at least the communication is clear. This level of communication gives you a certain level of freedom. You are free from thoughts, like who needs to know this information versus that information, or do I tell this group of staff some information about the company and not tell this group. But better yet, you are free to communicate everything, and you no longer have a burden of information that you are unsure who needs to know what.

I am not saying that you need to tell all of your secrets to everyone, nor am I saying that you need to share proprietary information with everyone. I am saying in the course of the day-to-day-operations of your business, your agency or your school you will want to establish that you will communicate clearly and often the expectations of the company, the vision, mission, and core values of the community, and the expectations for all staff to meet in order to win at your vision.

Smart Process #4: Being decisive when beginning again, is very important, and here, I share information about decision-making that is helpful when you want to begin again differently. I was at a seminar where someone was trying to sell those in attendance a financial packet. As a way of getting more of us to buy, the presenter shared a quote he attributed to Bill Gates. Now, I do not know if Bill Gates actually said this, but the quote makes sense, and I am in agreement.

"Successful people make decisions quickly."

I don't believe in making hasty decisions, and I do not believe that this quote is telling us to make hasty decisions. I do believe that to be successful, you cannot wallow and delay when making decisions. I believe successful people are decisive people, and if they make a decision that doesn't work, guess what? They go back and make a different decision, and they move on.

Smart Process #5: Focus on reflection is one of the most important processes to learn when beginning again. The quote, "The more reflective you are, the more effective you are," became our rallying cry as a team as we began to think through every aspect of every day of our work to make sure we were becoming more effective as our thinking improved. We now have this quote representing one of our core values. We believe that reflection is so valuable at our company, that all of our team members are required to deliberately schedule a time to reflect daily. We do not set the limit or cap, the team member does. Now at our company, it is a deal breaker when someone does not reflect daily. We are changing into a more effective agency, therefore we make sure we are thinking critically about everything as we grow and expand. We reflect because we are all vested and we want the best for our company. We believe I am a success if you are a success. If someone on the team is not reflecting and growing, then I believe they are stunting my growth as well because we depend upon each other to become more effective.

Smart Process #6: Focus on the importance of motivation. When I had my epiphany that morning, I believed God spoke to me, and I immediately began simultaneously listening to Joel Osteen daily. Joel Osteen has one of the largest congregations—nearly 90,000 members—in the world. He has been accused of being the smiling preacher because he loves to smile. He has been accused of a lot of other things, too, but I am accusing him of being the most hope-filled person on our planet, as every one of his messages—and he has hundreds—brings hope to everyone who listens.

Every Friday our team has a standing team meeting that we call Minnie's Motivational Moments and most of those Friday's we focus on a hope-filled message from Joel Osteen. All of his messages are on his YouTube, but he also has a SiriusXM radio station at 148, but you don't have to subscribe to anything to hear a message of hope. I believe his messages helped me greatly as we were waiting to hear the news regarding our request for funding for our new plan in 2016. Instead of talking about this opportunity in the uncertainty of "if we get funded," we all began to use the terms "when we get funded." We believe we were speaking by faith and prophesying or being mystical. We believe words matter, so we talked differently, and I attribute a lot of the positivity we experienced through what I was learning by listening to Joel Osteen.

Smart Process #7: Focus on the importance of having the right people and treating them well and a focus on money. Money is not evil but necessary. We can have a conversation about money without focusing or falling in love with money. Money is how we will be able to begin again to serve our communities differently—our customers, clients, and others—so we will want to make sure that we have clarity regarding our finances and begin again to appreciate budgeting and make decisions regarding money. Do I advocate no debt to run businesses? Absolutely, I totally believe like Dave Ramsey teaches in his baby steps; however, this is your business, and I believe we can still have a great discussion about financials even if we agree to disagree about debt.

Following these Seven Smart Processes, every day consistently will guarantee that you do things differently and that you begin to win again. I also added at the end of each chapter a smart process idea from team members who have shared thoughts about what has worked for them by being a part of a company that has decided to do things differently.

Begin Again Differently (BAD) Thought:

Think about and write down your hope for tomorrow and predict which of the Seven Smart Processes you think you will begin tomorrow.

Chapter 4

SMART PROCESS #1—BELIEVE

*"The future belongs to those who believe
in the beauty of their dreams."*
—Eleanor Roosevelt

What will it cost you to believe? Or what will it cost you to stop regularly beating yourself up mentally about your failure or your loss? Is it too expensive to believe? Is it too hard? Especially since you blame yourself for your loss and you can't stop thinking of what has happened to you, your company, your family and possibly others. Is it too time-consuming with everything else that is happening in your life to stop and believe?

Smart Process #1: It Takes "Belief in Hope" to Begin Again Differently

I believe that you can have what you want happening to your business by actively believing. I am not just spewing positive messages. I believe that when you believe, you are taking positive actions to regain control and begin again. The caution I would share here is to be deliberate about what you believe you want to happen. It is not right to believe for someone else's business, house, spouse, etc. But it is right to believe the best for your business, house, spouse, etc.

Believing is a positive action, therefore can negative people begin again, without believing that they will be successful again?

I am sure that they can. However, I don't hang around negative people, so I am not sure what they are doing. There is a verse in the Bible that says that the sun shines on the unjust as well as the just, so yes, I guess negative people can begin again and have success. If this is you and you have a propensity towards negativity the first step you will want to do is change.

I am not saying believe for hope's sake; I am saying believe for your sake.

What in the world is wrong with having hope amid despair?

Who made it unpopular to be positive?

Are you scared of people asking you, "Why are you so happy when you should be sad about your lost business, contract, marriage, job?"

I believe that when people believe something good or bad, it usually happens to them.

To get started on your road to begin again, let's agree that Henry Ford had it right when he said, "Whether you think you can or can't, you are right." Henry's quote said another way would be something like "whatever you believe you can or can't do, you are right.

This Henry Ford quote sounds like it is up to you to decide to believe. Therefore, to begin again, you must be willing to think you can.

No *ands* and no *ifs* and no *buts* about it.

Thinking you can begin again is winning half the battle of beginning to do things differently. With your belief in yourself, you will be ready to weather the storms that come from making major changes in your life. You can do this! Since you are still reading, I believe you have accepted the fact that you can do this, too.

Let us also agree that beginning again, once you believe in you, will not happen overnight. You will not suddenly have extra money. The contract you lost will not magically reappear simply because you are ready to start over again differently. Taking one day at a time is a crucial step to consider when you begin believing again. Being patient with the process of beginning again differently is a vital mental aspect on the way to your comeback. Are you normally impatient? Great! All you need to do now is change.

Believing You Can and Wanting to Change

There are lots of theories, methods, and approaches to change. The approach I would like to share is that change begins when you decide that something is more important than not changing. You will choose to change when you weigh the way things are now—you're impatient—to the way you want to become—patient and able to take one day at a time.

There is a beautiful Christian song about taking one day at a time. The concept is essential, because even if you don't get it and don't agree with taking one day at a time, you really, quite frankly, don't have a choice. Do you disagree with that statement? Do you think you have other options besides taking one day at a time? There is no time travel happening for real, maybe in the movies, but not in real life.

I really should share a disclaimer here about me. I tend to see most things in black and white. Especially those things that seem non-negotiable. When I write in this chapter that you have no choice but to take one day at a time, I really believe that. No matter what is going on in your life right now, there is no way you can get to tomorrow any quicker than living out the next hours until you go to bed and get up the next morning. Even if you go to bed earlier than usual because you can't wait until it is tomorrow, you still have to wait on the sun to rise before tomorrow comes. So why not decide to live each day to its fullest? "Whether times are good or bad, happy or sad..." (from Al Green's song *Let's Stay Together*).

I remember being about thirteen years old when a deacon from our church and his family picked my sisters and I up for a ride to a Wednesday night Bible study class. I was excited and blurted out as I was getting into the car, "I can't wait until Saturday for the fun festival to happen." The deacon stopped, closed the door to the car and would not let me in until he finished scolding me. He said, "Don't you know you just wished two whole days of your life away? Do you know that tomorrow is not promised, but you just wished that you could skip Thursday and Friday?" When he finished, he let me into the car, and I said, "I'm sorry."

Later, when I reflected on why I remembered this incident from so long ago, I really believe this incident had a part to play in helping me be patient with things, situations, and, to some degree, with people in general. When I think about the fact that, because we do not know what tomorrow will bring and we do not know what will happen tomorrow unless someone has some psychic powers or insight into the future, you really have to wait until tomorrow to happen to find out what will happen.

Wishing for tomorrow or any one day to hurry up and come will not make that day hurry up and come. It may cause you to miss some learning, growth, or opportunity that could have come your way that you didn't recognize because you were so focused on tomorrow or any other day but the present. What's my point with this story? Part of the need to believe that you can change by taking one day at a time will help steady you as you begin the process of beginning again. See, you do not know if this process will take a long time. Will it take two months or six months; one year or two years? Since you don't know, nor can you know how long any of this will take to get you back to where you want to be, being willing to be patient as you work through this process will be immensely important for you.

How long will this process of beginning again take? I believe it is different for everyone; however, for the record, even though we live in a microwave society where everyone and everything appears to be going at lightning speed, change takes time. To get the most benefit out of the process, your commitment of time is required.

This is what I know for sure. The day I jumped out of bed and realized who was really in charge is the day I began to change. I allowed change to occur every day after that, and I have continued to change so that I can continue the work of beginning again differently so that we never ever lose another contract that could stop us from fulfilling our dreams.

I am not saying that any of this is easy to do. I believe a lot of hard work is ahead of you, but when I tell you that my life began again on the day I jumped out of bed, free to let God lead and guide so that I could follow, it seemed like it got more comfortable to go to work every day knowing that I was changing. Even if I did not see the changes, I knew that I had decided to change, and I believed that it was happening. You know what else? It was great not knowing everything when people would ask me what our next step was going to be or what were we going to do. I felt great saying, "I don't have a clue, and I believe that God is leading us and guiding us." Even if they looked bewildered at me, I felt great. I remember one time, another business person came into our office asking when we would be selling everything so that she could come back and get our furniture. At first, I was struck by the insensitivity of her question. How dare she assume that we were giving up and about to sell our furniture? Why didn't she ask how she could help us out instead of asking how she could clean us out? But all I said was that I had no idea, but we'd let her know when we knew. For the record, we never sold or loss any of our office furniture, our materials, nor our property. We owned all of our buildings and equipment without any debt, and we have kept everything as we have worked towards the process of beginning again.

Will people be insensitive to you and what happened? Absolutely! While Americans are usually known for rooting for the underdog, a lot of us like to kick people when they're down. No doubt you've been kicked, and it does not feel good, because usually when you're down and out, you don't have the energy nor the strength to kick back. But no worries, once you begin again and begin to rise again, those people who kicked at you will know that their actions did not cause you to give up your belief system.

The Big Deal about Hope

Believing in the change that you will need to make as you take one day at a time will be much easier when you have hope. Whether you're a fan of Joel Osteen or not, he has become one of America's top voices on having faith when things seem hopeless. I don't reverence the man, I reverence the man's messages about having hope. I listened to and used Joel's' messages to help me begin again differently.

I do accept that people have their own opinions about faith and hope. I know that people have preferences for speakers and different leaders. Joel is the leader that I believe God sent to me to help me keep my mind focused on hope rather than what was surrounding me every day as I began to do things differently.

Until I started listening to Joel, I don't believe I realized the importance of having and using hope to win. After I got up that morning knowing that I no longer was in charge, who was I going to put my faith in and how was I going to put my hope to work? I knew that I was now ready to allow God to run every aspect of my life. I knew that I had been a Christian before my failure, but I now knew that I had not always, consistently allowed God to be the Lord of my life in every aspect of my life. I tended to allow God to be in charge when I thought I was over-my-head, but when I thought I was right, I plowed full steam ahead without acknowledging God in all of my actions. Now I knew that I would do things differently, and I began to check in with God on every little thing just to make sure I was following his guidance in my everyday life.

I knew that I could read the Bible, but when I discovered Joel Osteen's station with new messages every thirty minutes, I listened consistently. What I heard astounded me. All I heard was hope in every message, the underlying theme seemed to be,

"Have hope in God that He will provide, show you the way, be your guide, never leave you alone, be there for you in thick and thin, keep His promises to you as you continue to praise God, and pray to God to lead you and guide you, you can have hope that He will because He will."

While I knew of Joel's ministry over the years and had seen him on television, this new way of hearing him every day changed me. My schedule now was to wake up between 4:30 a.m. and 5:30 a.m., hit the button on the phone for SiriusXM, and sit back and listen. From that day in early February 2016 until the day we received our massive $54 million five-year contract, I heard Joel every morning for about thirty to ninety minutes (depending upon how early I awoke each day). I listened to Joel going to work; if I traveled, I listened to Joel on the road. I found out that I could not listen to Joel at night because he would put me right to sleep. But early in the morning, his messages of hope helped me navigate, letting God run my life every day without interference from me. Joel's messages during this time resonated with me because of what I was going through, I really believe that God had me find SiriusXM station 128 so that I could be helped by the hope messages that I was hearing.

One of the messages that helped me early on was #447. This message focused on having a good opinion of you like God has a good impression of you. When you hit rock bottom, and no one has a good impression of you, it is sometimes hard for you to think good things about yourself. This message hit me like a ton of bricks as I realized my failure did not need to prohibit me from thinking of myself positively because, after all, I was still a child of God, whether or not I had failed. This message also gave me confidence. Having confidence helped me to continue to embrace the change that was happening and helped me rise a little bit more every day.

I was learning and accepting the fact that my failure did not have to strip me of my confidence. I was still a human being worthy of love and respect, and I began to act differently and not hold my head down just because I had failed.

Message #448 focused on understanding your value. It helped me to value who I still was in spite of my failure. Again, I learned that there was no need to undervalue myself due to a failure in my life. It is easier to put yourself down when others are putting you down, but if you know your true value and what you have to offer, even after a loss, you do not have to lose hope that you have no value left to offer. I learned and began to understand that you do not have to devalue yourself after a loss.

Message #543 says not to settle for good enough. Before I suffered the loss, it pains me to admit, but I really felt that mediocrity was okay. I did not have a reliable standard by which to measure what we were doing, so I was always changing based upon whatever I heard at the time was important. I was just happy and content, at the time, to keep our head above water. I believe now in hindsight that I was just settling for whatever was good enough at the time so we could get by and start another year. Even though others might look at me now and not believe this about me. I know that I really did make allowances and excuses throughout the years for mistakes and mishaps that happened along the way. I know now that I did not always hold others nor myself accountable, as I should have for the work we were doing, and this probably played a part in our loss.

As I listened every day to Joel's messages, I began putting the number of each message that spoke to me in the notes section of my phone. I began playing some of the messages for our entire team during our weekly team meetings so they could hear and learn from them like I was learning from them. One of those messages was #427, *Excellence in the Workplace*. Our team now listens to this message every year to remind us that we have been allowed to do work that matters excellently to glorify our creator. Another message that our team listens to once a year is #581, *Keep Growing*. I'll talk more about the lessons we are continuing to learn in the chapter on motivation.

Do you have to listen to Joel to have hope? Absolutely not! Did it help me? Absolutely! Do you have a different source that may help you change your thoughts about having faith and believing that you can begin again? Then, by all means, utilize your source so that you can consistently change as you begin again differently!

Finally, as my hope grew, I believe I began to become more confident in what I was doing to begin again differently. I really grew and became more self-assured that I was on the right track by beginning again differently. This was a great feeling, and one I continue to cherish each day.

Begin Again Differently (BAD) Activity #1:

Go to YouTube.com, type in "Joel Osteen," listen to any message for three to five minutes, and write down 'hopeful thoughts' you hear. Write down what you think you have heard that may have given you another reason to start having hope. Or please listen to your favorite motivational speaker. Write down what you are hearing that is giving you hope. Read what you've written down about hope at least once each week as you begin to do things differently.

Current Team Member T. Grant's Reflection on This Process:

"Being deliberate about believing and having hope... has become real for me. We often get a false sense of self with past accomplishments. Going into a new and different environment allows you to reevaluate yourself and your beliefs. I stepped into this workspace that was completely unfamiliar, without knowing what to expect. Doing this has allowed me to believe in others and to trust the process."

Chapter 5:
SMART PROCESS #2—FIND YOUR NOBLE GOAL

*"People and organizations who know their why
enjoy greater, long-term success, command
greater trust and loyalty among employees and
customers, and are more forward-thinking and
innovative than their competition."*
—Simon Sinek, from his introduction in *Find Your Why*

Smart Process #2: Take the Time to Discover Your "Why"

When I lost our major contract, I had plenty of time to think. When I rediscovered Simon Sinek's TED Talk on the golden circle, where he introduced the concept that "businesses need to know their why first, before knowing their what and their how," I deliberately took the time to rediscover why our company existed and to re-evaluate if our "why" was still relevant and important. I also had to face the truth and think about whether our "why" was still important to the community as well as to me, our company's team members and our Board Members.

I began answering the phone at work throughout several weeks and inadvertently questioning callers about our business and "why" they were reaching out to us even after we lost our contract. I also began having different kinds of conversations with different team members regarding our company and what they thought was important about our why. It did not take me long to accept that our why was important enough to try to begin again differently.

Yes, I got the answer I had hoped for, but I believe I was prepared just in case I discovered that our company was not important enough or relevant enough to warrant investing in beginning again differently.

I believe that this is one of the most important processes anyone can take to when beginning again after suffering a loss. This is absolutely one of the most important things I did when I had plenty of time to think after losing our contract. I believe one of the mistakes I made when I failed and lost our contract is that I lost track of our agency's why.

I definitely did not have anyone on my team knowing our why; nor were we living our why. In fact, I would suggest that we all had different whys as to why we were working together, or why team members were on our team. As the leader, I had failed in the past to communicate that we all needed to have the same why to be the agency we wanted to be. I believe before losing our contract, we had already lost our why or our purpose for being the company we had started eighteen years earlier. Thus, losing the contract was a culminating event that actually occurred years before when we lost, or no longer were living with, our why.

I had heard of Simon Sinek's work on discovering the "why" and his Golden Circle TED Talk that had ten million views, and I had even shown our team members the video as we watched together during a team meeting, but I did not understand what the true significance was. As an ineffectiveness leader at the time, I showed the video and told our staff that all we needed to do was what Simon said and that was the end of the meeting because I did not know how to lead us effectively to implement Simon's Golden Circle in our company.

What is Simon saying when he says that "people don't buy what or how you do what you do, they buy why you do what you do?" Now I know that Simon is saying your why has to be the most important part of your business if you want to grow and expand as you begin again. Knowing the importance of your why and being able to communicate your why to yourself, your team, and then to others, including potential clients or customers will help you begin again.

To put it simply, you must have a purpose for living to be fulfilled in life. Simon shared that he discovered the power of "why" when he stopped and realized that he was just "meandering through life as a consultant". He stopped one day and realized that he needed a purpose in order to be fulfilled in his existence.

Once I understood that knowing our purpose for being a company was important towards beginning again differently, I immediately planned the agendas for our staff meetings to only focus on our remaining staff working together to reestablish our mission, vision, and core values.

I am connecting the need to find your "why" to being the same as identifying your "noble goal." I think of your noble goal as the reason you were put on the earth. Your "why" then is your noble goal or your reason for living. This, to me, is the same as finding your purpose for living. Rick Warren wrote a very popular book that sold over thirty-four million copies titled *The Purpose Driven Life*. In the book, Rick shares the three major reasons God put you on this earth and helps readers determine the answer to the question "what on earth am I here for?" I am hopeful that you can agree that there is a great need to be purposeful about determining your noble goal or your why as you make the decision to begin again differently after suffering your loss.

Mission, Vision, and Core Values

The words mission, vision, and core values are used frequently in a lot of entities and businesses, and a lot of support has been given to the fact that everyone individually should have a mission and vision for the life that they are living. I agree that having a personal mission and vision is important. I also agree with the line of thought that says it is important to determine your personal mission and vision before working together with people on a collective mission and vision for the agency or business you are running.

I believe that you will want to establish your mission for the company business first. Working on the vision for your mission, purpose or why I consider your second step. Finally, you will want to determine the values that will represent how you achieve the vision you have. One consultant group helps entities develop their mission and core values simultaneously and then they save the vision work for last. I believe that you will want to do what works best for your company as you begin again differently. I want to encourage you to do what feels best or most comfortable for your team to do. The most important thing to do is to be deliberate in stopping to do mission; vision and core values work with your team. You will not end up with a mission, vision or core values if you don't deliberately stop and make it a priority.

In our recent work with 250 school staff including teachers, principals and Superintendents we noticed that ninety-nine percent of them were struggling to implement our program. When we finally shared our thoughts about their struggles with them, we all agreed that the struggle to implement the program was based in part to the fact that none of them had reviewed or revisited their mission, vision and core values in several years leading up to implementing our new program.

In fact, several of the school staff shared that they did not have a mission, a vision, or core values. The program we were implementing with the schools had various complexities that required alignment to what the schools were doing. It was soon evident that the gaps that began to appear were because schools were attempting to implement the program without having clear school missions, visions, and core values. The clarity came when there were some chaotic moments during the implementation, some misunderstandings and a significant lack of clarity regarding expectations. Our company immediately contracted with a company that agreed to assist each of our schools with developing mission, vision and core values.

I am encouraging you to encourage each individual on your team to decide what their personal mission and vision for their lives are simultaneous as you work collectively to create a mission and vision for the business. I believe that this will help your team make relevant and meaningful connections when your company creates or recreates the mission, vision and core values going forward towards beginning again.

This is a very time-consuming thing to ask you to do and it may seem like fluffy work instead of concrete work to get you back on track in business. I believe that taking the time to work with your team on the mission, vision and core values will prove invaluable to you in the future. I want to recognize with you that this is a very time-intensive activity and that you will want to plan it so that your team sees the commitment you have to involve them in helping to shape what the company is becoming as it begins again differently.

Some of the people I continued to work with during the time of our loss were people I knew were not going to continue with us past the school year or for the long haul. As Jim Collins says in his book, *Good to Great*, you must have the right people on your bus, and they must be in the right seat on the bus. As we met regularly, I could tell that there was some resistance from some staff; however, I was determined to ensure that everyone had a voice in what our mission was to become. At the same time, I knew that some people would eventually leave and not continue working with us because I could tell that not everyone was aligning up with our new mission and vision. I had learned, however, that it was important to ensure that every employee had a voice and input into helping to create the mission, vision and core values.

Whoever you still have on your team must be involved in helping to create or revise the mission.

Don't want them involved? Then let them go.

There is an important Bible verse that says a house divided against itself cannot stand. This means that people working together who do not agree or have similar mindsets can cause the house to fall apart. Eventually, I knew that people who should not be on our bus would be weeded out at the end of the school year or whenever they found other jobs. But until then, they were required to participate in the mission work we were doing to reestablish our mission.

Why didn't I just let them go as I came into the realization that they were not right for our company? I think I kept people for several reasons…

- **Reason (or Excuse) #1:** It was going to be difficult to hire educational staff in the middle of the school year as most educational staff are hired before the school year, not during the school year. We also wanted to disrupt the lives of our parents and students as little as possible during what proved to be the last year we would be a school.

- **Reason (or Excuse) #2:** So many of our staff had left us due to our loss, and at a minimum even if these people were not right for our company long-term, they were serving a purpose at the moment.

- **Reason (or Excuse) #3:** I was still becoming more effective at doing things differently, and I did not know how to let them go in a way that respected them and our company. I had begun to look at things differently, but I was still new at the beginning again, and I simply did not know how to let them go even though I knew that they needed to move on to other companies.

Your mission is a way to communicate why you exist. Your vision provides you with what your company will look like when you live your why. Your core values dictate how you want to live each day as you work towards achieving your mission every day.

As I mentioned in Chapter 1, as we were going through the process of losing the contract, we discovered that our nonprofit did not have its own mission, vision, and core values. The work we began to do was to create the mission, vision and core values for the nonprofit.

It really was a lot of hard work, but rewarding to peel back our agency and look at what we wanted to become as we looked together at what we wanted our mission and vision to be, now that we were virtually starting over to begin again to figure out our why. This time, I wanted to make sure that we, and not just I, were significantly and meaningfully involved in our mission so that we could all own whatever we determined our mission and vision would be.

I thought about not sharing our mission in this book because there is a tendency for people to copy other company's mission statements. I realized though that I already share our core values later in this chapter and I shared how we developed our vision so I decided to include our mission in the book as an example of what we determined our company's noble goal; 'why' to be. The mission statement of our organization took several twists and turns over lots of months. We continued to work to refine our mission as we continued to begin again differently. Also, I have to give credit again to Simon Sinek for the way in which he articulated his 'why' because we copied his format of using the word *exist* in the way we formatted our mission statement.

YES, INC.'s Mission:

"We exist so that children have effective educators. We help educators become more effective!"

There are some resources on our website at yeseep.org that may help you get started if you've never done mission and vision work before. When I began working with my team, I really wanted to hire a consultant to help us flesh out our mission and vision, but I had been in so many trainings in my past, I eventually decided that I had the confidence to led our team through the work of creating our mission, vision and core values. I thought that it was also important for me for my staff to see me leading us to this new understanding. As I had been the leader that had lost the contract, I now needed to be seen as the leader who was leading us back to where we could begin again more differently.

Yes, this was hard and uncomfortable, but it was important that I did not pass this important task to someone outside of our business, so I was surprised when I took the time to lead that my staff responded with a mission and vision that we eventually finalized together. When I met with our board of directors later in March of 2016, our board members enthusiastically approved the work our entire team had done to recreate our mission.

Technically, it would have been important for me to work with our board of directors first, and then have the board share the mission and vision with the staff to get staff input before having the board of directors approve the mission and vision that we all now would have had input into creating. However, my entire board of directors lived out of the state of Texas, and getting them to do the work that I eventually did with the staff would have been logistically difficult and taken much longer to finish. In March of 2016, I was able to have our board of directors join us in Houston to review the work that the staff had done. With our new mission and vision, we then began working on our core values.

The process of taking time to get your mission and vision and core values right is more important than rushing to get something on paper so that you can say that you have a mission, vision, and some core values. It is more important to make sure that you have something that is of value to you, that means something to everyone who will continue working together as you begin again differently. You will want to make sure you have a mission that represents 'why' your company exists that everyone in the company can agree with.

For instance, if you have a company that repairs HVAC units, your company's mission may be something like, "We exist so that our customers' HVAC units work exceptionally well after we've repaired them." When you have your team members memorize the vision so that they live the vision every day, when they go to repair a customer's HVAC unit, you will know that they will not give up while they're in the field, no matter how tough the HVAC unit is to fix.

I had a plumbing problem in 2011 in my house that was ten years old, and I could not get hot water in the master bathroom that was far away from the water heater. The repairman assured me that he would not give up until I had hot water. He returned to my house on five different occasions and assured me each time that he would not give up. Finally, he was able to locate the issue with the line to my bathroom, and I remember thinking when I felt the hot water that the company must have had a great company mission because they kept their word and did not give up until I had hot water. I decided that I would always call that company back whenever I needed plumbing work.

What is a core value? I believe when you have core values, you have traits that you, your staff, and board will emulate and live so that when you are working with clients and customers, they will notice how you represent yourself.

There is no certain number of core values that you need to have. Doug Miller, the author of *Storybrand*, recommends having a number of core values that employees can remember. He shares his optimal number of core values is three. When I initially followed Dave Ramsey and his Entreleadership program, I wanted to have all of the core values that Dave had. However, a lot of his core values did not match up with our business, and Dave was stressing to us that we needed to make sure we had core values that represented what we believe, not what other companies believed. So, we stopped as a team and spent several weeks working together to create the values that would represent how we planned to live and work together as a team to fulfill our noble goal and our vision.

As you read about our core values below, I want to stress that our company is not perfect, and neither am I. We constantly struggle and fail forward to live the way our core values dictate would require. Yes, it is disappointing to us when we mess up from time to time. What is really most important here is that we have values to help us set the bar for the way we want to live and each day we are striving to hit the bar.

- **Integrity**—"We continuously practice what we believe." In Dave Ramsey's book *More Than Enough*, he focuses an entire chapter on the value of having integrity in business. When we began our core value work as a team, we started with the importance of the company and all team members having integrity. We are working hard to always and continuously *say what we mean and mean what we say.*

- **No Gossip**—"We take negatives up, and positives all around." I know that this is a value that a lot of businesses have trouble with, and I've been told on numerous occasions that it is not possible to have a no-gossip policy because everyone gossips, so "you're being unreasonable to think that you can get people not to gossip."

But, again, I was inspired by Dave Ramsey because his company has consistently, for the past eleven years, won best workplace in Nashville, and when his team members are asked questions about why they like working at Ramsey's Solutions, they are very clear that they like coming to work not worrying that gossiping will be happening around water coolers or in whispers. The like coming to work being able to focus on their work and not the personal lives of the employees. Dave says if the IT department messes up, you don't want to have the printing department saying things like, "those knuckleheaded IT people don't know what they're doing." You want the printing department to go to the head of IT to help fix the problem. When people stop talking negatively about others, but rather seek to solve issues, business is done in an environment that compliments everyone who is working rather than tearing down other people.

I told our people that it was important to take issues *up* and not to others because trying to complain about something that does not fix the problem. I believe we all know that when people gossip, it is because they can, and they may not want to have a problem fixed, as it is so much easier to complain. I encouraged our team to make sure that our focus is on fixing things rather than complaining about things. Now when anyone thinks someone is gossiping, he/she immediately holds them accountable and directs them to the right person to get their needs met in a positive manner.

- **Clear Communication**—"We believe to be unclear is to be unkind."
- **Failure Leads to Success**—"We believe that learning from our failures leads us to success." Failure leads to success is my favorite core value as I have cherished the way I have succeeded by using my failure to help me. It really is true that when you embrace your failure (what you've learned from your failure) you can realize

the greatest successes. I have also heard many people say that they have learned much more from their failures than any of their successes.

- **Reflection**—"We deliberately think about our thinking in order to continuously learn and grow."
- **Modeling**—"We demonstrate what we expect from others and ourselves."
- **Self-Employed Mentality**—"This is not a JOB. We do work that matters to all of us."
- **Team**—"We are team members, not employees."
- **Humility**—"We focus on others more." (From Patrick Lencioni's Book *The Ideal Team Player.*) We actually added this core value after reviewing Patrick's work within his book and deciding that we agreed strongly that having humility as a core value was important to our team.
- **Smart**—"We get people." (From Patrick Lencioni's Book *The Ideal Team Player.*) We added SMART as a core value for the same reason that we added Humility.

It is important to say what your business stands for when it comes to the character that you want your business to have. Will your business make promises it cannot keep? Will your business hire and fire people without regard to how you would want to be treated? What about integrity? Will your business have integrity, or will you do what you were taught in business school, that the fittest are the only ones who survive?

Saying what you will and won't do and meaning it is super important, and quite frankly, something I had missed during the eighteen years I was leading before I lost our contract.

When an insurance agent came to inspect one of our buildings, the maintenance guy said that if the agent knew that the building was not vacant, our premium would be as high as $49,000 each year. Before I began working on really understanding what integrity meant as a core value for our agency, I agreed with my maintenance man as he worked to hide the fact that we occupied the building. However, after letting God lead and guide me in everything, the next year, when the insurance agent came to inspect the building, I told my maintenance to absolutely not lie like he had done the year before. And you know what happened? The insurance agent did not ask any questions, nor did he want to inspect the building. I don't believe he even visited the property. For some reason, the insurance agent's priorities were different than they had been the year before. I really believe that having confidence to stand by our core value of not lying to the insurance agent was a test that we passed as we were beginning to really think through how to live our core values.

I do not believe you have to stop working altogether to do your mission, vision and core value work. I do want to emphasize the importance of getting your mission, vision and core value work in front of your team as soon as you can so that they know that you believe it is important to communicate the mission, vision, and core values together. Creating our vision took several months of meetings that last four hours so that by June 2016, we had our vision flushed out. Our mission was flushed out sooner but went through several changes as we revisited our 'why' numerous times from June 2016 through November 2018. We had a mission but as we are still beginning again differently, we allowed ourselves the luxury of making sure the mission was working for us. Our core values work was completed within a month with our team working two hours each week on finalizing what would become our ten core values. I hope that you will embrace the time it takes to allow you to continuously work to communicate with your team that your mission, vision and core values work is important to the future of the company as you begin again differently.

A Word About Goal Setting

> *"A goal properly set is halfway reached."*
> —Zig Ziglar

I ran out of time to include in this book all of the valuable information I have learned over the years about the importance of having goals. Though, I really didn't always implement what I had learned until after my business loss. I now had plenty of time to think and when I heard the information about setting goals as originated by Zig Ziglar, a successful author, businessman and motivational speaker, I decided to lead our team through several sessions about setting our personal and our business goals. I, soon, realized that goal setting would be an important part of our journey each year of beginning again differently.

On our website at yeseep.org, we include the information that has helped our company create and review goals every year. We have learned from a review of what Zig created that there are seven goals everyone would be wise to create each year and there are five characteristics of each goal that will determine if a goal can be achieved. For more information that can be helpful as you revisit goal setting visit yeseep.org.

Smart Process Connection from a Company Team Member:

During our company-wide morning meetings, we revisited the core values to ensure we were living what we said that we were doing. One day we decided to have our company complete a twenty-one-day gratitude challenge. Each day team members were challenged to write three things they were grateful for, showing gratitude to something new each day.

As the team worked their way through the more general things to be grateful for (family, health, a roof over their heads) it became more and more of a challenge to see things that are not commonly viewed as something to be grateful. Being grateful for traffic because it means you have a vehicle to get you places is another level of gratitude, and this challenge was able to get us there.

At the end of the challenge, we took the time to write a team member a message about why we were grateful for them.

Scientists have proven that one of the greatest contributing factors to overall happiness in your life is how much gratitude you show. Opening up the door to sharing gratitude with one another was a beautiful way for our team members to embrace why we were able to work for a company that allows team members to show and represent what it means to be grateful.

Begin Again Differently (BAD) Activity #2:

Watch Simon Sinek's entire TED talk on the Golden Circle. Then decide what part of the circle you understand the most. Finally, write down your understanding to see if you can document your noble goal, or what your "why" is.

Current Team Member T. Warren's Reflection on This Process:

"Understanding that every breath I take has a purpose gives me a better understanding of why I am here."

Chapter 6:

SMART PROCESS #3—OVER COMMUNICATE

"When in doubt, overcommunicate."
—Dave Ramsey, Entreleadership Mastermind Event

Smart Process #3: When In Doubt, Overcommunicate.

The beauty of overcommunication is that you do not have to think about something later wondering whether or not your messages with your team members have been received. When you overcommunicate, you guarantee that you have communicated everything you know at the time about a topic to your team. Overcommunicating means as well that you have answered every question to the best of your ability, and you have provided as much clarity as you have at the moment. You can now sleep at night knowing that you don't owe anyone anything related to whatever your expectations are regarding the information you communicated. This works whether you are communicating new salary information, new bonus information, introducing a new concept or business product, or anytime you are communicating to anyone.

When I heard about the value of overcommunicating, I decided I wanted everyone at our company to know everything. When I read through Kip Tindale's book about his company The Container Store, I agreed that we want our communication at our company to be "daily execution of practicing consistent, reliable, predictable, effective, thoughtful, compassionate, and courteous communication."

The only thing I seek to be careful about communicating is individual compensation, however, I share my compensation, as I want everyone to know what he/she can aspire to as we begin again differently. I don't mind sharing my compensation because I believe in the power of numbers. When I hear numbers, I get inspired and motivated so I share my individual numbers with our team as a way of sharing if I can do and earn this, so can you.

One of the major ways humans are different from animals is the ability we have to communicate with spoken language in the way we can think and speak. Words are important. Proverbs 12:18 from the Bible says that words can cut like a knife. Another verse shares that words can give life or give death. These are some very strong realizations about the power of words.

We use words every day to communicate all kinds of things about how we are feeling, what we are doing, what we like and dislike, what we are thinking, how we want certain things done. We use words to describe everything from the landscape to the painting we just saw in a gallery or on a wall or in a store to the clothes people wear or the way people comb their hair. Words are everywhere! Because we can talk and use language to express feelings and expectations, words are vital to communicating why, how, and what we are beginning again differently to accomplish.

With an English Language degree from Chicago State University on my resume, I thought I was a great communicator. But when I lost the contract, one of the things I learned was that I was not as good of a communicator as I thought I was. I remember going into a meeting with staff at the end of the workday several years before we lost the contract with some important information that I wanted to share. Everyone waited for me so that they could go home. It was a Friday, and everyone had plans. I came into the meeting. I shared the information that was vitally important to share, and then, as I finished, with about five minutes left before everyone would bolt for the door, I asked for everyone to tell me what I just said. I believed that I was clear.

One by one, I asked each of the almost twenty employees who were in the room that day what I had said to them. As the first person shared, I listened. Then about ten others shared before I stopped and let everyone go home. No one—and I mean absolutely no one—shared anything remotely close to what I thought I had communicated to them. Eventually I got over the initial unwarranted anger at the staff for not getting a clear understanding of what I thought I had communicated. I did not say anything to them as they left. My heart sank because I spent several quality hours preparing and getting my thoughts together so that I would be clear, and there was no one to fault but myself for not clearly communicating exactly what I wanted to share.

That experience taught me something very valuable about communication. It is the person doing the communicating who is responsible for presenting a clear message, painting a word picture, and for making sure that the audience gets it. It was unreasonable for me to be angry with staff for not understanding my message because I was the one communicating my message. While I did not get the full extent of this lesson until several years later, the incident stuck with me in my mind as a reminder of the fact that the messenger is responsible for the message.

What I learned, much later, in October of 2016, right after we had been awarded our big $54 million, five-year contract, was that it is important when communicating to overcommunicate. Now, before you go in your mind somewhere else, stay here for a minute. What I learned is that overcommunicating works. It works because it lets your audience know exactly what is being said. It works for the messenger because there is a certain level of freedom that comes with getting a clear message out of you no matter what your message is. It works for everyone. Overcommunicating is not the same and should not be confused with telling all of your business to anyone who will listen, or just talking for the sake of talking. However,

However, I believe that overcommunicating is ensuring that you have communicated your message one hundred percent so that no one leaves not knowing what is expected. This type of communication also confirms that you will avoid your team members having *parking lot conversations*. Parking lot conversations usually occur after a meeting where people gather outside near their cars and talk about what just happened in a meeting because there was a lack of clarity regarding expectations provided during the meeting. Parking lot conversations often lead to gossiping among team members. At our company, we discourage parking lot conversations deliberating during our meetings because we focus on getting clarity with everyone in the meeting. Whether in a one-on-one conversation or with a small group or a large group, I have come to value the ability to overcommunicate.

Sometimes, no matter how much you overcommunicate, you fail to get through to the listener because the listener is not really listening to every word you are saying, because they cannot or won't let themselves listen. I heard an example of this in a story Dave Ramsey told about when his company Ramsey Solutions went through a major reorganization. Because his company meets every Monday in a staff meeting with all 200 to 300 staff members at a time, he used the Monday staff meeting to tell everyone about how he was restructuring his company.

The first thing he said, and he said it often, "No one will lose his or her job. This is a leadership restructure due to our growth and no one, I repeat, no one will lose their jobs." But lots of people in the business world have been reorganized out of positions and jobs when companies have restructured, so some people on Dave's team did not hear Dave as he repeated this information every Monday for about twelve to eighteen months. It took a while to complete the restructure, so they quit, probably thinking, "Here we go again, let me start looking for another job."

Dave admitted that there wasn't much he could do for people who could not get over the restructuring due to their past. I do not believe he lost a lot of people, but he was amazed to some degree by people who listened to him every week as he confirmed for them that he was not lying and that they would not lose their jobs who still left the company convinced that they would be laid off as a part of the restructuring.

You can do everything possible to have a clear message, to repeat yourself often and to overcommunicate, but you cannot make people listen. People who have had bad experiences with whatever you are communicating about may not hear you because their mind is clouded by the past experiences as soon as they hear trigger words like "restructuring."

The morning after I jumped out of bed and realized God was in control was the beginning of me becoming an overcommunicator. Over the course of a few days, I had to meet with all eighty-three employees to tell them the progress of our fight to save our school and what was most likely in store for them regarding looking for another job. Because information was public about what we were going through, I wanted to be the one to communicate the truth about our agency's status instead of our employees hearing about us only on the news.

I had eight different departments of staff to meet with: bus drivers, custodians and maintenance people, teachers and teacher assistants, nutritional/cafeteria staff, office staff, and administrative staff. I had to schedule the meetings at different times due to the different work schedules because bus drivers started at 5:00 a.m. and some staff and other staff worked until 8:00 p.m. covering after-school programming. As I met with each department over a period of four to five days, I began to get more and more confident about how I was communicating what essentially was bad news about our contract as a charter school was.

In the past, when I had communicated, I communicated only what I thought was necessary at the time for several reasons. First of all, I did not want to bog anyone down in details that I thought they probably did not need, or I thought that they could not understand. Secondly, I was very concerned that they would worry about things that they could not change. Finally, I did not want to have long meetings communicating information I thought they could not handle or that would leave them with more questions than answers.

I did not overcommunicate in my past life before my loss. However, as I found myself overcommunicating confidently and consistently with the different departments, I noticed that I was becoming a stronger, more effective communicator.

It is true, you improve when you do something consistently. I felt great even though I communicated bad news. It really felt great to get everything out of me. I felt like I carried a huge burden. When I chose to overcommunicate everyone knew what I knew about the loss. This action had all of us all being accountable for the information and not just me.

Around this time during one particular department meeting with about nine bus drivers, I shared that our efforts to save the school were not working, but that we were not giving up, and everyone should be aware that we would not need bus drivers next year.

One bus driver asked, "So are you telling us to go look for another job?"

I said, "Exactly."

During my communication with the bus drivers, I did not want to start with a negative statement like, "You all need to look for another job," but I was absolutely sharing that they all needed to look for other jobs. In my past life, I would have tried to soften the blow a little bit and I might have said something like, we're continuing to fight and we're hoping for the best, but the minute the bus driver asked and I answered, I felt free.

"Yes, no one will have a job next school year and yes, you need to take care of your families so yes, you need to look for another job."

I also made it clear that we needed everyone to just give us a notice if they found a job so that we could plan to take care of their duties since we still had about three to six weeks left to finish off the school year. This is an example of how I was beginning to follow the golden rule that later would become our vision of treating people the way I would want to be treated if I were to face the same kind of situation.

Weekly Team Meetings

As I began learning how to begin again differently, I learned about overcommunicating consistently by having regularly scheduled, non-negotiable team meetings. It was difficult initially to change from being inconsistent with our team meetings to be consistent. I had always thought that I had good communication skills, but I also knew that if anything came up, and I mean anything, I would cancel or reschedule a meeting so that no one knew when and if we were meeting due my inconsistency. So in order to change, I met with staff to inform them that going forward, whenever we said we were going to meet, we were going to meet no matter what. It still took several months for us to be consistent, but everyone knew that we were striving for consistency in our meeting schedule.

The next thing that was difficult was the messaging that needed to happen during these hour-long staff meetings. I struggled with what we were to meet about. What was I supposed to be communicating? Again, I turned to Dave, but his company was so much bigger than mine. I was concerned at first that maybe copying Dave might not work, but it did. Our staff meeting, I learned, was supposed to be about our business—the status of our business, the finances of our business, the mission, vision, core values of our business, the expectations for our team members about our business, and a host of other topics that needed to be overcommunicated consistently to our team weekly.

In order to ensure that all of our team was beginning to understand how we wanted all of us to live our mission, vision, and core values, we needed to meet often to review together so that we would all get the same understanding regarding the mission, vision and core values.

I remember learning from my Harvard professors in 2008 during my summer course work on the *Art of Leadership* that some research indicated that you usually have to tell someone the same thing over and over again—at least ten to twenty times—before they hear you. Then I learned later that, once they have heard you after ten to twenty times of repeating yourself, you need to repeat yourself again another ten to twenty times so that they can now understand what you are saying. This information helped me as I shared with staff over and over how we were changing and what our expectations were for everyone to change with us.

Again, initially this was difficult, as I had never been consistent with regularly scheduled weekly hour-long team meetings, plus I had to keep changing the time until I found the time that worked for us. We now meet from 8:30 a.m. to 9:30 a.m. every Monday and Friday. We train educational leaders as a part of our business model, several times during the summer months, so there are a few times when we may have to reschedule because we conduct training sessions throughout the summer months. However, for the most part we meet bi-weekly, fifty-two weeks out of the year.

This level of communication has been one of the most rewarding benefits I have experienced as I work with our team members. We all seek to get a daily understanding of what is expected of us to continue beginning again.

I can also tell that our team is benefitting greatly just like I have. I recently received an email from one of our team members mentioning that she had nominated us to be recognized as the small workplace of the year. I had often looked at this recognition over the years in the paper wondering if we would one day be there. I had also often wondered if, by chance, I might nominate us, but then I would think of the negativity we had with some on our team and that it would probably not be a good thing to have the negativity be a part of this. When I received the email from the team member telling me what she had done,

I knew whether we won or not, we had already won with her nomination of us.

For now, we meet two times per week for one hour. Dave calls this "working on your business." Both working on your business and working in your business are two very important tasks. Usually as business leaders, we tend to focus on the end goal (bottom line… profit and loss), meaning we tend to put a greater emphasis on working in our business.

Through using these smart processes, I really began to embrace that it was as important for me to work on my business as it was for me to work in my business. I began communicating this fact to our team regularly. I needed them to know that our meetings each week were for us to work on our business so that we can grow and become more effective when we leave the meeting to go back to working in our business.

We meet every Friday morning from 8:30 to 9:30 A.M. as a part of working on our business. Monday's meetings are about our business status and updates regarding our projects, our calendar, hiring, our why, our noble goal, our vision, and our core values. Friday's meetings are about motivation. I decided to name our Friday's meetings Minnie's Motivational Moment, when we recreated our mission and vision in 2015. This name was inspired by what I I had learned from being raised by Minnie Lee Higgs, my mother. As I thought about how we were beginning again differently, I thought this was a great way to honor my mom's memory by naming our Friday meeting after Minnie. For the record, I believe my mom was born first, so Minnie Mouse, Mickey Mouse's love interest, does not own this name. In any event, we stop every Friday morning to check in on how we are living now with what motivates us. I talk more about this in chapter nine.

One-on-One Meetings

Each week one-on-one check-in meetings occur with each team member and his/her team leader. This has become one of our most important communication processes. Every one of the thirty-four people who currently work for our company has an opportunity to further communicate expectations and understandings with their team lead so that we provide effective services to our 250 teachers, principals, and superintendents in twenty different school districts and campuses.

No one on our team leads more than five people. Each team member is scheduled to have a fifteen to thirty minute one-on-one with their team lead to focus on communicating expectations, as well as to communicate the growth of each team member. Each team member, at a minimum of one time per week, is required to identify a growth goal to work towards for the next two to three weeks in order to ensure that everyone in the company is growing.

I lead our core team of five leaders and our senior leadership team of two members and myself. Each week I find out how their team members are growing and learning as well as I am made aware of any of our team members who are struggling.

Recently I began the practice of having virtual standing meetings each Monday through Friday beginning at 8:00 A.M. with my team leads. These standing meetings have given my core team and I more opportunities to align our thinking and our expectations with what we plan to accomplish daily. These standing meetings have become growth sessions for all of us as we take the time to discuss critical factors impacting our ability to be successful each day. Usually we are on the phone for an hour and we start our call while driving to the office.

Consistent daily and weekly communication is one key way our team is learning and growing together because we constantly overcommunicate to ensure that we have an understanding of what is expected of us at all times.

Finally, one of the major benefits of overcommunicating is the fact that everyone involves usually ends up with a great understanding of what has been communicated even if everyone is still in disagreement. At a minimum, everyone understands. Biblically speaking, "In all your getting, get an understanding" (not an agreement) is our goal.

Smart Process Connection from a Company Team Member:

I have been at the company for almost three years, and I have been a witness to what happens as our team continues to grow and learn from over communicating. We deliberately role-play our ideas and thoughts before we start any project or we have to communicate new and difficult information to others. This looks like us taking on the roles of our customers as we practice our messages and how we want to be perceived especially when the message may not be positive for the customer.

One example of this process was when we had a very high-level executive at another company implement incorrectly one of the processes that we require. We wanted to make sure that not only did the company executive get the expectation from us correct, but we wanted to make sure that we did not offend the executive by correcting her. We spent several days making sure our written communication to the customer had been accurate and clear regarding what needed to be corrected.

Then we spent several days role-playing our conversation with her to make sure we were following our vision of treating people the way we wanted to be treated. This level of overcommunicating by taking the time to make sure our communication met our agency's core value was time well spent. When we finally had the conversation with the executive what we thought was going to be hours and hours of convincing her to change actually took less than ten minutes.

Our deliberate focus on having communication that was clear and covered all areas (overcommunication) made us feel great once we had achieved our goal. The executive not only improved but became one of our best customers out-performing others that we were working with.

Begin Again Differently (BAD) Activity #3:

Make a list of up to three difficult conversations that you have not communicated yet to a team member, family member, or friend. Choose one of the three different conversations and talk through with yourself how the conversation might happen. Feel comfortable yet? Then schedule a time without a time limit to have the conversation. Afterward, write down your thoughts about what went well and what didn't go well, and prepare for the next conversation. When you do something consistently, you get better and better.

Current Team Member T. Wilson Reflection on This Process: "Overcommunicating is a skill. Often, we say some and assume the rest is understood without realizing it. I've been able to get my point across and help others get theirs across to me by enhancing this valuable skill."

Chapter 7:
SMART PROCESS #4—MAKE DECISIONS

"The most difficult thing is the decision to act, the rest is merely tenacity. The fears are paper tigers. You can do anything you decide to do. You can act to change and control your life; and the procedure, the process is its own reward."
—Amelia Earhart

Smart Process #4: Begin Daily to Get Comfortable Making Decisions

Don't like a decision you've made? Make another decision.

Have you heard the quote attributed to Ronald Reagan that we make over 800,000 decisions every day? Can you imagine making 800,000 of anything, much fewer decisions?

93

Really? I got tired just thinking about making 800,000 decisions. Most of the decisions we make are subconscious decisions, like putting your left foot first to go up the stairs followed by your right foot and other decisions that we take for granted we are making unless we don't have feet. If we do not have feet, then we are probably making decisions more consciously of how we are going to get around, but I think you get the point that throughout a twenty-four-hour day, all human beings are active, whether consciously or not, making decisions.

As I thought through everything that came from losing my contract, I deliberately focused on how, when, and where I was making decisions, and I realized early on that I was a wimpy decision-maker. I was so wishy-washy in almost everything that I began to say no wonder I had this or that problem. I rarely made decisions that I could communicate clearly to others.

I changed as I began again by learning to communicate differently when it came to making decisions, and I learned rather quickly that it was okay to make bad decisions or decisions that turned out to be wrong decisions, the point was to be decisive, even if you find out later you were decisively wrong about whatever decision you made.

This change caused people to look at me twice sometimes when I shared a decision because I sounded different. To me, I sounded firmer, but to others, they said I sounded mean or angry. So I began to communicate and overcommunicate that the way I was changing meant that I was becoming more decisive in my decision-making, and while I may sound mean or angry, I am not. I am just attempting to be strong in my conviction that the decision I just made is how our agency is moving forward now.

It may change tomorrow once I get new and different information, but until it changes, we will be doing this action, training, work until I make a different decision.

Being decisive and making decisions is an important part of beginning again differently, because now you are communicating clearer and you have mission, vision, and core values. You and your team want to make decisions about who you are becoming as you change.

As I mentioned earlier regarding core values, I had to make a decision that it was important enough for us to stop and take the time necessary to finalize our core values. Basically, we had been very excited that we knew our mission, our why and our vision, however, I soon realized shortly after beginning again differently that we were going to have to STOP and finalize what would represent our core values. I made a decision that we would utilize our time for our next week's morning meetings to flush out our core values. I had to decide that working on our core values was important enough for thirty-four people to stop and do for two hours each week until we finalized the ten core values we have now. This decision meant that our focus shifted for about one month while we completed this important work.

For me, I was seeing so many opportunities as I was walking with God as my guide, and I got excited about every opportunity I saw. For example, at the time, one of our team members was at the top of her game in child nutrition programming. In fact our charter school at the time was the only charter school in the state that made a profit on our child nutrition program, and I gave all the credit to our child nutrition director. While you can't really make a profit off of a federally funded program, what the state allowed us to do was to have up to three months of reserved funding without being required to return the funds. They expected us to utilize our reserve funding to upgrade equipment like stoves, refrigerators, freezers, and dining areas, and even though we were careful to make sure we only had three years of reserves, it was a challenge each year because we made money on our child nutrition program every year.

We had low costs and overhead, and a majority of our students received free or reduced lunch because most of our students qualified as low-income families. When I looked at our resources, I thought, maybe God is going to have us write contracts for other schools to run their child nutrition programs. I knew that what we achieved in our program was not limited to just us, and that I could utilize our child nutrition director's knowledge to help other districts. I reached out to other districts to find out how much they made on their child nutrition program, and none of the districts were making money. Most of them were paying from the student fund to supplement the child nutrition program. I said, "Yes, I have found a goldmine."

As I talked more about this in staff meetings and other places, people asked me questions like, "Are you saying that you are going from running a school to running a child nutrition program?" I would reply, "I really don't know. Wherever God says go, we will go." In retrospect, I believe God was showing me that I could be successful with any venture and not to limit myself, but I am very glad that God did not open doors for us to become a business doing child nutrition programs. One of the districts I spoke to has already begun to do things differently just because I spoke to them about how much money they were spending on their child nutrition program from the student funds, and they are now preparing to implement their own program and save the extra $30,000 per year they were spending out of their student funds. So even though we aren't in the Child Nutrition Program (CNP) business at that time, we were able to help another school out just by sharing our thoughts.

What's my point? You will want to make decisive decisions about who you and your company are becoming, and if you make a bad decision that doesn't work, just stop and make another decision. Please be encouraged to explore the options that are being presented to you and be okay with making a decision that you may need to change later.

Henry Kissinger said, "The task of the leader is to get his people from where they are to where they have never been." In my case, I was leading my people to a place I had never been before either. I relished exploring all of the opportunities that seemed viable at the time for our future. I had no idea as I began taking one day at a time where God was leading our company. I had faith as I began making decisions following God's leadership and faith provided me with daily comfort as I began making decisions differently than I had made before losing our contract.

It Is Important to Make Decisions

Eventually, you will want to finalize what you want to do or be as a company because you will have made the decision not to give up and not to quit. You will want to utilize your mission, vision and core value work to guide you in your decisions regarding how you are going to begin again. You will want to take the time to make decisions and to change decisions that need changing. You do not want to make decisions in haste.

> *"You will decide each day what matters most*
> *for your time, for your team, for your company*
> *and then proceed to follow through to stay focused.*
> *Have a conscience and listen to it."*
> —Henry Kissinger

Sometimes, it is okay to take the time to sweat the small stuff because it can be the small things that can cause you big problems when they are left unresolved. We often overlook little problems and issues when we're in trouble or struggling because the bigger problems seem overwhelming. However, the bible clearly states that 'the little foxes destroy the vine' (Solomon 2:15). To me that means that letting little things go unresolved can lead to destruction. By this I mean you will want to focus on all of the things happening to you during the time that you are beginning again differently, even if you think they are insignificant.

Help all of your team members become heavy lifters of your mission, vision, and core values. You learn to make decisions together. I am not advocating that you need to engage in shared decision-making with everyone. I believe the leader has a priority to make decisions. Period.

Becoming a leader that is willing to do things differently will mean that you will want to have a focused intensity on utilizing all of your resources and your team members to resolve issues instead of trying to lead from inside a vacuum. You will not want to nor will you most likely be able to form committees to study every issue before a final decision is made. As the leader you are charged with and accountable for the decisions that you make whether you involve others in your decisions or not. However, you will want the freedom that comes from leading collaboratively when you involve and include input from others in the decisions that are made. I believe the research is very clear "top-down leadership" does not yield long-lasting results.

As I began again differently, I began explaining and communicating more with my team about the way I was changing as a leader regarding decision-making. I wanted them to know and understand that I was allowing God to lead me, and that I would be making decisions by sharing information with them, allowing them to share their thoughts with me and then making the decision I thought was best for the agency. I made their roles clear to them by saying, "I value your thoughts and opinions, but, when I make a decision, it will be based upon the information I know at the time, and on the way I believe God is leading me. It will not be based upon your thoughts and opinions. I want to hear your thoughts and opinions just like I want you to hear my thoughts and opinions. When I make a decision, it will be based upon what I believe is best for the agency and our team."

I wanted to have this kind of conversation with our team because in the past I was and I was perceived as being a "lone ranger," leading by myself. I no longer wanted to be perceived as having all of the answers or perceived as making all of the decisions in isolation from the team."

I confirmed for my team that I would not be asking them to vote on decisions that I planned to make and we would not always be in consensus on every decision that I would be making. I wanted to assure my team that as I am the one responsible for the decisions I make in the company's best interest, I no longer wanted to make decisions in isolation anymore as I did before the loss.

What I have just described above was different for me but not difficult. Now, what I love about decision-making is the opportunity to reverse any decision and make another decision if I need to for the good of the company. This is such a ridiculously fun and easy thing to do, but this (reversing decisions) used to trip me up all of the time. For some reason, I felt like if I made a bad decision, even if I knew I needed to make a different decision afterward, I did not think I could or should make a different decision because leaders are decisive. Right? I agree that leaders must be decisive, and I also now realize that you are being decisive even if you have to reverse or change course with a decision. This realization has been so freeing for me, and I know that it can work for you too when you allow yourself the discretion to make and then re-make decisions when you need to, depending upon what you are trying to accomplish within your business.

Recently I made a decision that led to the creation of another component of our program that led us to keep more individuals working towards becoming effective educators. This decision was an example of what can happen when you decide that making a decision is important rather than 'letting the chips fall where they may'. Several individuals did not qualify for our program at the end of our training over a period of four months. But we did not want to dismiss them due to the hard work that had been accomplished by them. Instead our team stopped and decided that we needed a way to keep the people involved so that they could continue participating even though they did not qualify for the full benefits of the program. We decided to create a new term, because they did not qualify as resident teachers, we decided to identify them as pre-resident teachers. They were able to keep working towards becoming a teacher, but in a different way. Making decisions can cause you to become more creative in your business and could lead to greater success when you are deliberate about the reason, purpose and importance of your decision-making.

One of the best decisions I believe I made early on in our company's development as we were beginning again differently was to approach one of my core team members about the discrepancy I saw in how she was communicating. Here's the story.

I was watching and listening to Deedee and Sally have a fun discussion before the start of our weekly core team meeting. They were laughing pretty hard and having a good time as they discussed the results of their recent personality profile where they both had been identified as high "C's". Being a high "C" meant that they were cautious in all of the ways that they communicated and made decisions. They were really gloating at the fact that they took their time to do everything cautiously and never made missteps because they were so cautious. The minute I stopped and really listened to them, I began to get disturbed because what I heard Deedee praising herself about, I saw as the opposite.

You see Deedee had been on the team when we lost the major contract. She had been one of the team members I had actively encouraged to look for another job so that she would be ready when all of our funds would be gone. I had watched her go on interview after interview without her having any success in getting any job offers. I remembered that I had even offered to coach her on interviewing effectively but she had declined my offer. I remembered quite vividly talking with her right before she was to participate in another interview for a position that she lit-up with excitement about when she spoke. I was really pulling for her but, again, she did not get the job.

Now as I sat listening to her gloat and praise herself for being a high "C", I became more and more convinced that I would need to say something to her because while she was describing as her good traits I was listening and thinking that those traits were hindering her growth and development as a team player. You see I had been watching and listening to R. Rogers for several months as we were starting over with the new contracts, and I had become quite frustrated by her "cautiousness". She was always, I mean one hundred percent of the time, never providing any immediate feedback. She took so long sharing during our meetings that I would often have to return to her for a comment after hearing everyone else share regarding issues we were discussing. Even when I met with her during a one-on-one discussion, she would always delay in answering or responding to any question or request for comment.

As I sat listening to her and her teammates discuss being a high "C," I made the decision that I would need to have a tough conversation with her during our next one-on-one.

Here's what I said, "Deedee, do you remember when you and Sally were talking about being high "C's" the other day before our team meeting?"

Her face lit-up as she confirmed that she remembered having a great conversation about being a high "C".

Then I said, "I have something to say to you that may be difficult to hear but I know now why you never got any job offers when you were interviewing." Her smile went away. I continued, "You never got job offers because what you were considering as being "cautious", looked like to the interviewers as someone who is unsure of themselves, someone who does not know what to say, or someone who cannot answer questions quickly." "You probably looked like you lacked confidence because you never provided answers quickly."

Deedee stopped for a minute and replied, "But I was always thinking of the correct thing to say."

I continued, "But you probably looked like you didn't know what to say as you were saying nothing." Then I asked, "Did you ever say… 'Give me a minute to think." Deedee confirmed that she never asked the interviewer for time to think before answering a question.

I continued, "You also do the same thing when we are meeting together. You are always hesitant to speak or to share what you are thinking." "It looks like you don't know what to say and you are coming across like you lack confidence in sharing your thoughts."

After several long seconds, Deedee confirmed that she agreed that I was correct about her cautiousness not being cautious but rather something akin to her having some insecurities around whatever she was being asked or whatever information she was trying to share. She really was scared or afraid to just share her thoughts. Deedee also confirmed to me that she agreed that she probably never got any job offers during that time, because what she viewed as 'cautiously thinking of the perfect answer or response', the interviewer saw her as someone who did not know the answer to the questions being asked.

Deedee and I agreed that her next professional goal would be to stop hesitating to speak and to just share what is on her mind without any thought about what she thinks others may be expecting her to say.

Here is why I believe this was one of the best decisions I have ever made when I decided to confront Deedee with information that was tough to share.

The very next time we met for our weekly core team meeting, Deedee surprised everyone at the meeting with her keen insights, her great ideas, and her brilliant suggestions. Everyone at the meeting began to wonder, "What has happened to Deedee?" Everyone was shocked. I was shocked as well because of the greatness that I was hearing come out of Deedee.

Thinking back on that time, I remember being upset about the situation with Deedee. I began thinking that Deedee had stunted my growth and our team's growth because she had not been sharing her thoughts due to her thinking that her being cautious was some kind of virtue. Due to her thinking that it was not okay for her to 'just say what she was thinking when she was thinking it', she had really been depriving our team of her wonderful information and insights. I really began to see that her withholding information had limited our team from growing and changing as fast as we could because as a member of our team, she had not been giving us her all when it came to the many discussions and planning meetings we had been having.

When I realized this fact, I called a special meeting of my leadership team. Everyone at the meeting heard me say the following, "We must be transparent and overcommunicate everything to and with everyone on the team because we do not know how we may be able to help each of us grow unless we communicate what each of us is thinking while we are having our meetings and training sessions." Everyone agreed that it is important for everyone's growth to regularly share how we are changing and doing things differently so that everyone around us can change and do things differently too.

Deedee has gone on to become one of our most valuable team members and actually leads more projects than the other core team members. I believe Deedee is more effective today because she changed the way she was communicating and it caused her to become a more effective team member and leader.

My decision to confront her about her communication helped our entire company grow.

Smart Process Connection from a Company Team Member:

As a core team leader, I was having trouble making decisions. I constantly procrastinated. I did not reply to emails that needed a response. Fear of failure was my main reason because what if I responded the wrong way? I often waited until I could meet with the CEO to create an email response that she expected me to write.

There was one particular time that I recall we were preparing to start a program from our grant. One of our core values is to clearly communicate. We believe to be unclear is to be unkind, however, we needed to get this information about the expectations for the program out to our partner districts. Time was running out. Though we had already created several guidance documents and applications we had not sent them out because we were waiting for our CEO to approve. She was busy bringing in a new district into the program therefore, spending time out of town with them and working on other things. I would send the drafts to her but because she didn't respond. I simply waited. Meanwhile it was getting closer to our deadline for getting the program moving to get people in our pipeline for the upcoming year. Finally, my CEO contacted me and began inquiring about when we had sent the district Superintendents the information they needed to communicate with their staff to make a decision on whether they wanted the pipeline or not.

After a long arduous conversation with my CEO who was rightfully upset because I had waited to share important information, she inquired as to why I had not sent out the information even though it was in draft form to at least give the Superintendents a heads-up about the program. I had been sitting on the draft information for almost two weeks because of my fear of making a decision to send out information that had not been finalized yet.

When my CEO mentioned that all we had to do was make a decision to send out the draft as a draft, I saw immediately that I had made the wrong decision by waiting. As I was waiting afraid to send out draft information, calls had been coming into the

CEO about where the information was and that is what led her to call me and follow-up. My fear of failure kept me from making a simple decision to push the button and it led to undue stress from others who needed the information that I purposely decided not to share because it was not finalized and approved by the CEO.

I did mention that I had an arduous conversation with the CEO? Well, she said something that triggered me to begin to think about making decisions good or bad. She said, "So what if it's not all the information they need? It's what you *know now,* so give them that. It's a draft. We are learning and we won't always get it right." She also said, "It's okay if you get it wrong the first time." As a leader, you have to make decisions and when they don't work out or you need to do something different, you model for your team that you're not perfect, so they will be okay with making decisions. When people are waiting on something from you when you don't make a decision, you cause them to be in limbo. You can't expect them to make decisions they need to make if we can't decide to give the information that we do have.

What was my learning? As a leader you need to make decisions on what you know at the time and not wait until you think it's all "right." When others are depending on you to make decisions you make the decision with the information you have, then revisit, review and revise when you get more information.

Begin Again Differently (BAD) Activity #4:

Make a list of the last four major decisions you made regarding your business. Write down the reasons you decided as you did for each of the four decisions. Then review the decisions that you made. Were they the right decisions for your business at the time? Do you have second thoughts about the decisions you made? Do you want to change some of the decisions you made? Then make a decision to change a decision that you still have time to do something different by making a different decision.

Current Team Member Y. Gonzalez's Reflection on This Process:

"I ask myself how will the decisions I make impact others? I think about the consequences of my actions. Will they lead me to being a difference-maker for others?"

Chapter 8:

SMART PROCESS #5—BE REFLECTIVE

"The more reflective you are,
the more effective you are."
—Confucius

Smart Process #5: Working 'on' Your Business, Rather than Always 'in' Your Business Requires You to Make Time to Reflect Daily

One of the most difficult things I had to do when I began again differently was to stop *doing,* period. I realized that, through all of the actions and the doing, I had lost sight over the years of our mission, vision, our why, and our core values. I had been doing school (going through the motions of all of the requirements of running a school) for eighteen years—hiring teachers, training teachers, recruiting students, working with parents, creating curriculum and calendars, implementing systems, changing systems, responding to systems, reading and answering emails, creating newsletters, trying to please and make accommodations every day for over 2,192 days. I planned and d prepared during the summer months to be ready to *do it again when school started in the fall.*

To stop and just *do nothing* was important for me to learn so that I did not fall into the trap of just *doing* business. It was a little easier to *do nothing* because of the lost contract—there really was less to do—but it was still somewhat challenging to realize that I did not have to *do things.* Instead, I needed to learn how to just *think,* and I do not mean to think about doing but to really think instead of doing.

Okay, so I am not really talking about anything mystical, magical, or spiritual. All I am really saying is that, as I began reading leadership books on being more effective as a leader, I thought more about what I was thinking about, why I was thinking what I was thinking, and what I was going to be because of my thinking. Instead of feeling the need to be *doing things in the business,* I began to think more about the business instead of thinking that being busy in the business meant that things were okay with the business.

Every time I caught myself thinking about doing something, I stopped and refocused on my thinking unless it was time to stop and drive home, get dinner ready, work on a project or any other thing I happened to be doing at the moment. Yes, I kept doing what needed to be done, but the difference now was that I also was striving to spend a significant amount of time deliberately thinking, and not just doing.

Before my loss, I would say that I spent almost ninety-seven percent of my time doing or thinking about what needed to be done. Lots of people like to say about themselves, that they are movers and shakers, that "they get things done!" While I never really said things like that, I actually do believe that I lived like that continuously. I was always doing something.

Now, to just stop and not *do* was interesting for me, as I discovered there were lots of learning to do as I was discovering more and more about how to utilize these smart processes to begin again.

Can anyone really learn anything if they do not think about what they are learning? I understand that we all get better at doing something when we do it consistently and continuously. However, before you even begin to do something, don't you have to think through whatever it is to make sure while you are doing, you are actually doing it right? I really believe I was not growing professionally that much, or as much as I should have been while I was busy just … doing. I also believe I was functioning mindlessly, meaning that I was just doing what I thought needed to be done without much thought into how I was doing whatever I was doing. For instance, each day became the same kind of day—get to work, read communication, put out fires, answer questions without much help.

I am not saying that our company, for eighteen years, did nothing right or good. We developed and implemented lots of programs that helped many of people, but I did not have a mindset that encouraged me to think daily and deliberately about what I was thinking about. So I am definitely saying some of what we accomplished might have been more effective had I known what I know now.

> "The more reflective you are, the more effective you are."
> —Hall and Simerol

As I began to spend more and more time thinking, my reading and learning led me to grow as a leader. I deliberately became a better leader because I was not spending all of my time doing any more. How do I know I was becoming a better leader? Well, for one thing, I could tell that I was making better decisions. For instance, before, it might have taken me three to four months to change something that was not working out well, but because I was now thinking more, I was actually able to see things more clearly in our organization that needed to be adjusted or fixed sooner rather than later, and I usually had ways to adjust or fix stuff that made more sense.

For instance, our Monday morning meetings first started off at 7:30 a.m. because some, but not all of our staff, started at 7:30 a.m. This led to not everyone being able to be present, and having one hundred percent of staff at the meetings was non-negotiable. Then we adjusted work schedules to 8:00 a.m., and still, we had some problems with different departments and teams. Soon afterward, when we moved the time to 8:30 a.m. and changed our entire work day to 8:30 a.m. to 5:30 p.m., this proved to be better for everyone, and we've had this schedule for almost three years.

In December 2017, we discovered a quote by Hall and Simerol at one of our training sessions. It says, "The more reflective you are, the more effective you are."

We added this quote to all of our meetings, our trainings, our core values and plastered it everywhere. We also required our entire team to deliberately reflect every day. We were already using a time tracker we modeled after the Entreleadership materials to help us manage our priorities each day, and now everyone was required to add reflective time to their day.

Yes! Our team gets paid to reflect, because when our team reflects and becomes more effective, so does our company. Reflection is a required part of everyone's day for no less than fifteen minutes each day.

The bottom-line matters, so as someone becomes more effective because they spend more time reflecting, our entire team and our business will grow and expand. Again, not from the *doing,* but from the reflecting we *do* before we *do.*

I learned early on while I was transforming and beginning again differently that "leaders are readers." I had heard several conversations in the past about successful people and the number of books that they read. Then, when I listened to Dave Ramsey talk about how he requires the newly hired team members to read books during their ninety days of probation, I was hooked. I immediately ordered the same books Dave required of his team and began requiring all of us to read them so that we could learn more about how we wanted to live more effectively within the mission, vision, and core values we were establishing.

The books we have everyone read are listed below along with why I considered them important for our team to read. We use the learning from the books to reflect so that we are always growing into more knowledge about how to work more on our business to serve more people as a way of expanding to reach our noble goal.

- *Entreleadership*, Dave Ramsey: Dave paints the roadmap of how to utilize what he did to become successful so that anyone can do what he did to make his business successful.

- *The Go Getter*, Peter B. Kyne: I actually required my son to read this book when he was a high school senior. This book helps the reader understand the way someone who wants to succeed does not give up even when unexpected things happen.

- *QBQ: The Question Behind Question*, John G. Miller: I found this book before we lost our business, but because I was just going through the motions of doing; I required it to be read but never followed up with the staff at the time on what the book was actually promoting. I don't know if anyone read the book because we never stopped to review the book together. Now that our team is working together on personal responsibility, we reference this book all the time in our team meetings and talk about how we are using the concept of being personally responsible for our own actions.

- *Rhinoceros Success*, Scott Alexander: I reference this book later in Chapter 10 because this book helped us understand the value of being rock stars.

- *More than Enough*, Dave Ramsey: I like this book because of the focus on businesses having integrity. I believe this book is important because it focuses on the need for businesses to operate in integrity instead of just focusing on the bottom line.

- *Total Money Make Over*, Dave Ramsey: We give this book free to all team members as well as the Everydollar.com app so that our team knows that our company wants each team member to handle his/her financial business more effectively so that they can also handle our company's business. As a benefit to all employees, we purchased a subscription to SmartDollar. This program is really Dave Ramsey's online version of Financial Peace University. Each team member earns points as he/she completes assignments and watch videos describing the seven baby steps to get out of debt. This information is important. I stress to all of our team members that they can not be effective at reflecting or doing when they have bill collectors calling them and when they are worried about their debt. So now all team members have a certain level of peace as they work through the baby steps.

- *Business Boutique,* Christy Wright: We share this book with our team, but do not necessarily require it to be read by the team yet. I thought it was an important book to have for our team members because I, like Christy, am a woman leading our business, and her book is designed to help women run their businesses more successfully.

- *Retire Inspired,* Chris Hogan: I believe this book helped our legacy and helped me help our team members think about the future because we want to prepare with our current finances for whatever lies ahead for our families and us.

- *Complete Guide to Money*, Dave Ramsey: This is not required reading for our team, but we have this book readily available for all team members when they want a reference document regarding insurances, making big purchases, buying vehicles, setting up different investments and everything under the sun that has to do with money. Whenever I am planning a major purchase, I check out this book to see what Dave has to say about the purchase.

- *Legend of the Monk and the Merchant*, Terri Felber: This book is a book that shines the light on the fact that whether you have taken a vow of poverty as monks do, or whether you are making money in the marketplace, you still have a valuable part to play in our world. This book really helped Dave deal with the wealth he was accumulating because he started getting a lot of hate mail about money and he started getting lots of people complaining that he was greedy or money hungry. So this book helped Dave accept that it was okay to be wealthy and everyone in his company is required to read it, because he expects all of his people to grow financially like him.

One of the things I did differently when I lost our major contract was to stop and think when it was time to make decisions rather than proceeding ahead with some decision without thinking just because I was the decision-maker and the leader.

It was frustrating for my team members when I would stop because it usually meant a delay in what we were trying to accomplish, but I began to require all of our individual team members to just stop and focus intentionally on the issue at hand before making decisions in order to make better decisions.

I led team meetings where we trained on what it looked like to just stop and not do anything until a thorough reflective thought process had occurred, and then we proceeded cautiously in order to ensure that we were making the right decision for that moment.

One of the first trainings we conducted for our new team members when we received the huge contract in the fall of 2016 was on the value of focusing on the power of being reflective. People in general are mainly focused on doing as opposed to thinking. We often hear people say they are so busy; they have people to see, places to go, and things to do, as they run through their lives just *doing, doing, and doing.* I made sure to hire people who were willing to focus with us on being reflective. We have hour-long training sessions where we focus on some aspect of learning and growing, but never doing.

Now our company culture is to conduct sixty-second, written take-away reflections during and after our meetings because we want to ensure we are checking for understanding and always on the same page with expectations. This sixty-second, written reflection is required to be documented in every team members' individual growth plan (IGP). Then everyone is expected to review his or her reflective comments throughout the week, sometimes with their team leader, but always as a part of their daily time tracker for at least fifteen minutes each day.

Here are some of the conversation starters I use to help our team members learn to value taking time to reflect throughout each day:

- "You don't know what you're doing, so I don't want you doing anything just yet." All of our team members were and are still new to the company and the company got new programs that we had never implemented before, it was important for me that all of our team not rush in to just doing something, but to really be thoughtful and reflective about the work we were doing. All of our team members have plenty of important degrees and experiences, but I stress to them that because none of us, including myself, have never done this type of work before, we need to be very reflective each day to learn and figure out what 'winning looks like' BEFORE we starting doing any work. Yes, this meant we had a lot of training sessions and discussions, because it has been difficult for very accomplished people to stop and reflect before they do. Even though they talk about the struggles they are having with just reflecting, they really are learning to love working this way, because it has made the work we do more enjoyable because we are being deliberately reflective and this is causing us to be more intentional about our actions.

- You don't know our program, so you have to give yourself time to learn our new programs. This is another topic of discussion that ends up sounding a lot like the information above, except the focus on time. Why in the world is everyone in such a hurry to do stuff...

doing anything as long as someone's doing something seems to be important… and they think they're being successful because they are doing stuff. I believe there are a lot of people confusing action with success, and I know that when we failed and lost our business, there was a lot of activity, and we were not being very successful. Therefore, I stress to our team members that taking the time necessary to learn what we're doing is more important than us doing anything. And then afterward, they tell me how rewarding it is for them to be involved in learning because it is making the process of doing more enjoyable because they have a great understanding and awareness of why (our purpose) we are doing as we seek to fulfill our mission and realize our "noble goal."

Some other discussion starters are listed below as examples of some of the conversations our teams are always talking about to guarantee that we stay on track with continuing to make our company effective so that it doesn't lose everything again.

- I need to make sure you learn our mission, vision, and core values so that you can make sure you can live them, so that is your "do"—do learn and live the core values.
- You've been given ten books to read within ninety days to ensure that you have some higher level of support that will assist you in learning about our mission, vision, our why, and core values.
- For probationary team members It is more important that you become a thinker, because then when you start doing, you'll be a more effective doer.

As soon as our loss happened, I realized almost immediately that we cannot win again just by the act of doing something. We were going to have to learn some different. Again even though I insisted that reflection was our major task when we began our new contract, it was still very difficult for new team members to grasp the concept that reflection or thinking was more important than the actual "doing" of a job. They were all ready to do something and I was not allowing them to do anything until we had taken time to reflect on our work, our vision, our mission, the way we were changing, our core values and the books we were reading. Stopping to reflect was very important to me because I believed when I had lost our contract, it was due to all of the *doing* all of us were *doing* and we never took the time to stop and think about our work; we just keep *doing*. We had been doing for eighteen years and it was difficult to change.

What I found that helped me shape the reflective type of environment I was envisioning for our company were two very powerful articles around the power of thinking based upon some of the teachings of John Maxwell. We use the articles to help new team members change the way they think about thinking. We also use the articles each year as a way to review how our company is continuing to become more reflective. These two articles place an importance on the value of great thinking and how to engage in great thinking. It's safe to say this does not come as naturally as one would assume. It is a choice. The questions after each article were useful in helping team members discuss what was learned in the article. We do not distribute or email the articles until we read and think through the articles together as a team. Then we copy the articles or paste the articles into our *individual growth plans.* We continue to re-read and think through the articles throughout the year so that we are always conscious of our need to be reflective in order to become more effective. The articles were written Dan Black on leadership and are presented below in their entirety.

Article #1: The Value of Thinking

"One of the hardest habits a leader can have is to take time to think. This is because a leader's responsibilities and tasks require action and forward movement. Influencers can be overly focused on the everyday functions of leading or managing that they overlook the value of thinking.

Dictionary.com defines thinking as to "consider for evaluation or for possible action upon, having a certain thing as the subject of one's thoughts, forming in the mind in order to know or understand something, and to call something to one's conscious mind."

To maximize our leadership potential, results, and production requires initiating and forming the habit of thinking. Author John Maxwell says,

- Poor thinking produces negative progress.
- Average thinking produces no progress.
- Good thinking produces some progress.
- Great thinking produces great progress.

During a conversation, you can usually identify if the person you are talking with takes time to think. Those who think have fresh, relevant, and creative ideas and thoughts. They are people who raise us to a new level of thinking and toward positive change. You can clearly tell when a person does not take time to think, they have a difficult time solving problems, generating innovated ideas, or having fresh and new content. It's important to remember people are drawn to those who think because of the value they bring to conversations, meetings, teams, and work environment.

The bottom line is that you have to choose to engage and form the habit of thinking no matter how busy your schedule becomes. In Ngina Otiende post "Want a Powerful Life? Own Your Choices" she says, "The truth is, no matter what happens to you, you still have the power to choose. That ability cannot be taken away from you." No matter how busy we might become we should intentionally choose to separate from the busyness of life and leadership. To find a place to think, clear our minds, and Engage in Thinking. David Schwartz said, "Where success is concerned, people are not measured in inches, or pounds, or college degrees, or family background; they are measured by the size of their thinking."

Questions: Do you need to re-prioritize your responsibilities and tasks to include more thinking? What are some other characteristics of a thinker?"

After we review and discuss the questions and responses after Article #1, we then read Article #2.

Article #2: How to Engage in Thinking

"Author and Speaker John Maxwell says, "Great thinking produces great progress." If you want to be a more effective leader then you must engage in thinking. Being intentional about thinking can be challenging though. This is because you have to stop leading, separate yourself from distractions, and take time to think. Maybe this is why so many people and leaders do not invest in thinking.

However, there are many benefits that come when a leader engages in thinking. Some include:

- They have relevant and fresh ideas.
- They can better bring solutions to problems or issues.
- They are more effective in communicating with others.
- They increase creativity.
- They can produce more in less time.
- They can better adapt to the changing world.

Below are six ways that will help you engage in thinking:

1. Chose to think - Thinking always starts with a personal choice to think. Making the choice to think requires discipline in setting time to think and then following through with it.

2. Associate with great thinkers - I believe you become like the people you associate with on a regular basis. If you're around great thinkers, then you increase your thinking and gain wisdom from those who are already great thinkers.

3. Have an inflow of great thoughts - Having a personal growth plan can be a catalyst to great thinking. This is because when you grow and learn you gain better or even new thoughts. A daily inflow of great thoughts can ignite your thinking.

4. Have a place to think - This is one of the most important things to consider when engaging in thinking. One

of my personal favorite places to think is at the beach (I live about ten minutes away from the beach in San Diego, CA). I'm able to frequently go to the beach and engage in thinking. The important thing is to find a place that's that is free from distractions, so you are able to think.

5. Be able to capture your thoughts - What's the point of thinking if you don't capture your thoughts. Being able to place your thoughts on paper or digitally allows you to remember and go back to your thoughts at a later time. I personally use Evernote to capture my thoughts.

6. Have a place to unleash your thoughts - After you have taken the time to think and capture your thoughts then unleash them to your followers, tribe, community, or the world. This might take place through your leadership or in a blog.

Questions: How important is thinking as a leader?
How do you engage in thinking?"

These articles helped us learning to have reflective time as an important part of our company as we began again differently. Reflecting allowed us to learn how to work on our business more than working in our business. This has helped us to change and transform so that we can continue to experience the learning and growth we will need to ensure that we continuously do things differently. I am proud to say that reflective time is an invaluable time and is a norm for Yes Inc.

Smart Process Connection from a Company Team Member:

When I first started reading and reflection processes with my first group of team members, within two weeks I heard statements like, "I am not sure what my role is or what my job description is supposed to be?" "I feel like I am getting paid for doing nothing but reading and enjoying myself." "This does not feel like a real job to me!"

I continued and did not rush these processes. By sharing and giving feedback and providing daily guidance about their reflecting on what they did and learned. They slowly started to change. A different mindset developed and evolved towards becoming more effective with work and life. I could see these changes in the work they did, their answers to questions, the discussions we shared, and through the feedback I provided. I brought in a second group and the following year a third group and saw the same pattern, the experiences, the learning and growing were the same. Changing lives not only at work but in their overall world was a powerful thing.

My team members grew tremendously in the areas of leadership skills, their abilities to find better quicker solutions, and they discovered that they were living better-balanced lives at work and at home. No one complained about not having a real job anymore. Thinking and stopping to reflect while trusting the process was a key to living a more productive and happier life.

Learning to stop and deliberately take time to reflect during the day has enhanced my ability to look deeper into finding better solutions and making better decisions. Especially when I am faced with challenges both at work and in my personal life.

"Good leaders help people get better at their job.
"Great leaders help people at their lives."
—Chris Hogan

Begin Again Differently (BAD) Activity Number #5:

Assignment: Create an Individual Growth Plan (IGP) by writing down your reflections, your thoughts, your concerns, and other information related to beginning again differently. Then read your writings every day before you write the day's new reflective learning information. Do this for a week. At the end of the week, look back through each day to determine if any of what you have written has helped you to grow individually in any of the processes you've learned, in any of the ways you now view your failure, or anything you think is helping you to begin again differently. If you like what is happening to you, continue to use your IGP daily and weekly to continue learning and growing.

Current Team Member A. Radder's Reflection on This Process:

"I have changed my routine not only at work but also at home because I realized that both routines should align. I have noticed a shift in my past self to my future self. I have always enjoyed reading, but now I am eager to read. When I finish a book, I immediately start another book to keep this habit alive. I am more reflective both at home and at work. Reflecting has made me a better critical thinker because when I write my thoughts down, I can really think through my thoughts in their entirety. I remember what I thought more clearly than ever before. The process of reading and reflecting renewed my passion, motivation and mindset for growth. I was able to reevaluate my spirituality and focus on what matters the most. Now, I spend more time reading than I do watching television in my spare time so that I can exercise my mind and stay sharp."

Chapter 9:
SMART PROCESS #6—GET MOTIVATED

Question: How do you motivate your team members?
Answer: You hire motivated team members!

At our company, we stop once a week, right now it is every Friday, the last day of our week to celebrate, learn, share, and reflect about "what's our motivation". Our purpose is to continue to seek out how to best live so that we can achieve our noble goal on a daily basis. Saying our mission is our noble goal puts our mission on a pedestal to remind us of why we exist.

I began calling our meetings Minnie's Motivational Moments because of my mom whose first name was Minnie. She had such a wonderful influence on my ability to begin again differently through what I remembered of her and the character she modeled daily of how to live with a purpose and stay motivated by placing an emphasis on your life's noble goal or purpose.

When we first began to create our mission, goal, and core values after our loss, I went back to the way my mom had raised my sisters and I. While we were on our fourth training session on creating the vision, I was able to share my mom's life story with our team as they were developing our company's vision, because she ultimately exhibited the golden rule every day of her life. I love the fact that our team was able, at the time, while they were still in work sessions, to work together to create our vision around the Golden Rule, "We treat everyone the way we want to be treated".

Putting aside an hour each week for our entire team to stop and reflect on motivational moments has been life-changing for everyone on our team. What better way to be motivated than to reflect on your dreams and hopes for your future? Each Friday of the year, unless our team is in a training session or we have a holiday, our team is spending an hour together working together on motivating ourselves.

The lessons I learned from the messages I heard from people like Joel Osteen, Dave Ramsey, Simon Sinek, and many, many others have definitely helped me keep hope alive and provide a level of motivation that I did not know I even needed before my loss. Their influences have helped me shape, change, and recreate my own version of their best practices.

One of the activities we have each Friday is listening and/ or watching a thirty-minute video of a motivational message—

usually a Joel Osteen message. The last one we listened to really had an impact on us because it was called "Pushing People Up." If you've heard of the pay it forward movement, the pushing people up messages were somewhat similar.

One of the life-changing messages shared was when you push people up, make them shine, do good to them and for them, you get a return far greater than you put out. Doing good for others cycles around back to you. For the next three to four weeks, after we had listened to "Pushing People Up," when we would come together on Friday morning for Minnie's Motivational moments, everyone would either share an example of how they had pushed someone up, or how someone had pushed them up. This kind of conversation every week is motivational because, as we continued to reflect on and do our work, we were actually in a great state of mind as we worked because of the positive vibes that came from being pushed up or pushing someone else up. My team continues to practice the habit of pushing others up on a regular basis.

"What is your motivation?" This is a great question to continuously ponder as you do the work you've decided matters most to you. Currently, my motivation is witnessing the miraculous change happening to all of our team members as we continue this process of beginning again differently. Watching and seeing so much development and explosive growth as our team members are literally changing in front of my eyes and ears is extremely motivational. Another one of Zig Ziglar's famous quotes states, *"Your attitude, not your aptitude, will determine your altitude."*

I believe your attitude about worrying will impact your ability to do things differently.

"Don't worry! Be happy!" (Bobby McFerrin) What if you fail? What if you don't try, again to do something different? Worry never solved anything and worrying about what could go wrong with you trying again will not help you solve your business issues. While it is a normal tendency in our world to worry about things you cannot see, like the future, worrying never brought the future closer to you, as you still had to go to sleep and wake up in the morning before you could experience the next day, no matter how much you worried.

I believe that it takes quite a bit of self-discipline to control worry, as we seem to naturally worry when we don't know things like what's going to happen, our next steps, what may be facing us, what a decision may mean for us as we begin again. Another thing, I remember as I was growing up as the oldest child is how much I would often worry about my sisters even more so than my mom. I would quiz them with questions like "Where were you? Why didn't you call? "We were worried about you." I definitely will share that I have had an amazing transformation over the years since our loss, due to my realization that I was never in charge anyway. Now I take deliberate steps to not engage in worrying by focusing on utilizing God's guidance in all that I do. I used to cringe with worry whenever we got a call from the State because toward the end, it was usually something negative and the call would make me start worrying about things like, our future or what bad thing the State would do to us next, but not anymore. I am extremely happy not to be plagued by thoughts that could lead me to start worrying.

Now, I am free to reflect, learn, and grow without wondering and worrying about the future or anything else. Am I perfect at not worrying? No! But I am definitely actively guarding my thoughts to do my best to keep worrying thoughts out of my mind.

It Is important to Motivate Yourself

Why do we have to get sick with cancer and then wait to be in remission before we smell the roses and appreciate the sunset? Why not just experience each day as it is and enjoy everything that you can?

So many people have life-changing events that cause them to re-elevate their priorities, and they sometimes report that the air smells different now that they have a new lease on life. Why not find a way to motivate yourself every day before experiencing a life-changing event? No matter what loss you are experiencing, you are six feet on top of the earth, so you still have the day to experience, to grow, and to appreciate the time you have. With so many tragedies that happen daily around the world, I think we really understand as a people that tomorrow really is not promised to anyone.

I'm sure you have heard of the bombings in the hotel in Sri Lanka where one billionaire father lost two of his three children while they were having breakfast. I'm sure he, nor they, woke up that morning realizing that they would be gone soon. They did not get a chance to decide to smell the flowers one last time or watch the sunrise one last time. They actually did not know that it would be their last day on earth.

The truth of the matter is that none of us know when it will be our last day, so why not decide to enjoy every minute whether you're in the midst of losing your contract, your business, your spouse, your job, or your income?

Make a decision today that you will motivate yourself because you are still breathing and being able to breath is something to encourage you each day. Did you get a raw deal when you lost your business, your family, your job? Are you left with nothing? Was it unfair? You may have answered yes to each question above, however, you can also say that you're still breathing and that means you can enjoy life for another day.

During the eighteen years leading up to our loss, I realize, now, in hindsight that I was no longer enjoying trees, flowers, animals, or anything outside of my office because I went to work when it was dark before 6:00 A.M. each morning and I left work when it was dark usually after midnight each night. I never saw flowers or birds or sunsets or sunrises, and I believe when you miss nature, you miss the most motivational things about our world. Now I deliberately go outside and breathe. I'll watch and smell the grass blowing in the wind. Lately, I've been watching wildlife eat the left-over dog food that my dog Sally doesn't finish each night. The other night I videotaped a beautiful little fox enjoying some of the Kibbles 'n Bits and when he hurried away to the left, from the right rambled up a big, young raccoon who promptly finished off the Kibbles 'n Bits, so I videotaped him, too. Witnessing nature at work became the highlight of my day.

> *"The world goes on and every day is a gift from God,*
> *so why not enjoy the day?"*
> —Joel Osteen, from one of his 800 sermons.

Believe me when I say I know that it is hard to think about being motivated or being motivational during a time of loss. Especially when you did not want to lose your marriage, your friend, your business, your job, your health, or any other loss. I am not a bereavement counselor or coach, but I do know that there are stages that have been identified that everyone goes through when they suffer a significant loss. I am not saying that you may need to grieve during this time in your life. I am also not saying that you will never be sad, disappointed, or discouraged by your situation from time-to-time. Lots of emotions are quite okay to have, but when you dwell on the negativity and allow it take over your thoughts so that you become somewhat of a prisoner to your thoughts, you limit the possibilities you have to enjoy each day to its fullest. A quote from Voltaire sums up my thoughts around the grievance issue succinctly, *"Life is thickly sown with thorns, and I know no other remedy than to pass quickly through them. The longer we dwell on our misfortunes, the greater is their power to harm us."* Absolutely, we all have and will continue to have bad things happen, however, we do not have to let negative thoughts take over, stifle us, or limit us from enjoying the day or night and we definitely need to find the wherewithal to move on with our lives from whatever misfortunes have occurred. There is no requirement that we have to allow 'bad things' to stop us from moving forward with our dreams, our goals, and our missions.

Sometimes you have to motivate yourself. Remember the commercial where two actors stop acting, look at the camera, and exclaim loudly, "What's my motivation?" Apparently they had lost their motivation to do the scene and wanted their motivation back so that they could continue. I always laughed out loud when I saw the commercial because they seemed so sincere in needing their motivation to continue. I also think the commercial illustrates that we all need motivation to continue—to continue living and working and enjoying our world.

In high school, the girls on my track team began calling me *Amazing Grace* because I was a church girl and I always won my races even though, to the girls on my team, I was bigger and slower and should not be winning. Although I was bigger than most of them, I really was the right size for my height and weight, but to them, seeing me win was amazing. I remember thinking it was an odd name, but I embraced the positive nickname even though I did not think I was that amazing. What you call yourself can be very motivational. I never called myself by the nickname, but just thinking of the nickname gave me a great feeling and still brings a smile to my face.

I believe that it is important to your ability to begin again differently to find what motivates you and to utilize your motivational sources to help you be positive throughout your journey of achieving your dreams.

Smart Process Connection from a Company Team Member:

Our company stops once a week every Friday to have Minnie's Motivational Moment (M&M). We used to begin with a video and words of motivation. Something happened when I played one of my favorite songs "My Life is Fine" by one of my favorite singers, Mary J. Blige and I began to motivate our team through music by encouraging each member to dance a few minutes before the start of our meeting. Within the first three minutes of music each week, I witnessed our team enjoying the day before it even started. This turned out to be our theme each Friday; music playing before members enter the room so that they can dance down to their seat. This has empowered me as well as inspired all of our team members as we push each other up enjoying, and motivating one another before we start our workday. The days became much easier as we all were learning that we were all in this together.

We have now been dancing for almost two years during our weekly Minnie's Motivational (M&M) Friday meetings. This is now a norm for our team. During this time we have been to four different major Dave Ramsey trainings. We are now considered a "legendary company" because they look for us to bring the "motivation." We recently had a phone call with one of Dave's team members where she told us that we 'align perfectly' with their messages and they look for us to be at their trainings so that our motivational sprits can be shared with all of their attendees. We have been sharing this motivational norm with over 7,000 of Dave Ramsey's attendees. During one recent event, one gentleman in a wheelchair exclaimed that he had not had so much fun in a long time as I grabbed him up by his arms onto the dance floor and whirled him around. He laughed so much and we all had a great time.

Our company is proof that when you motivate your people, it motivates others and promotes joy. Because of who we are and the energy we bring with us we have been able to motivate the world around us no matter where we go

Begin Again Differently (BAD) Activity #6:

Think about and then write down what is happening around you when you feel the most motivated about beginning again differently. Write down the names of people who motivate you and reflect on what they do that helps you get or stay motivated.

Current Team Member R. Deleon's Reflection on This Process:

"As I began to lead my team and got to know them, I learned that while everyone's motivation is not the same, it is my job as a leader to find out how I can fan their flame. Everyone needs AIR: Appreciation, Inspiration, and Recognition."

Chapter 10:

SMART PROCESS #7—MAKE ROCK STARS

*"Always treat your employees exactly as
you want them to treat your best customers."*
—Stephen R. Covey

Smart Process Number 7: Make Sure that You Are the First Person on Your Team to be a Rock Star

Want to work with rock stars? Make sure you are a rock star first. After you confirm that you are a rock star, then you will want to begin the process of hiring people that you know can be rhinoceroses and not cows, as Scott Alexander coined. All of our company's new team members are required to read the book *Rhinoceros Success* by Scott Alexander. It is a fun little book, but it stresses the difference between being a cow and a rhino. Through Scott's book, all of our team members begin on their first day knowing what is expected of them, and our leadership team members begin having daily conversations with them regarding how they are becoming more like a rhino charging towards success rather than a cow waiting for success to happen.

Another focus our company has in order to ensure that we are all focusing on being and becoming rock stars is our intentional habit of always striving to learn new and different ways to push each other up. First of all, pushing people up does not mean that you allow yourself to be a doormat for people to walk on you or treat you less than you deserve as you allow others to be successful or to go first.

Sometimes people in the world we live don't do good things for others because of the thoughts that go through their minds that sound something like this:

- "I made my own way, so you have to make your own way."
- "Why should I do something for you to help you out? No one helped me out or did something for me, so why should I do something for you?"
- "If I help you, then you won't know the value of how you can help yourself."
- Or the classic, "What's in it for me?"

What does "pushing people up" actually mean if it is a good thing to do? Is it something like "pay it forward" when you pay for the drive-through order of the person behind you because someone paid for your drive-through order one day? Or you pay for someone's meal or pay for someone's groceries.

In this smart process of getting everyone around you to become rock stars, I think pushing people up is a little like the pay it forward movement, where random acts of kindness have now become a cultural nicety. I think we need movements like this that help our world with developing character around helping strangers. There have literally been thousands of positive stories around the pay it forward movement.

If pushing people up is not exactly like the pay it forward movement, and then what is it? I believe that when you push people up, you put their needs ahead of yours. I believe pushing people up is what Patrick Leoncini talks about in his book *The Ideal Team Player* as he describes the need for us to be humble. Patrick describes being humble as doing for others first. During our lifetime of the "me" generation, Patrick asserts that you want team members who genuinely are interested in each other, as well as the company, and not as focused on climbing the corporate ladder as they step on people's heads as they move up in the company.

When you push people up, you genuinely and generously provide what they need without regard to your own needs even if you have a need that is similar. This is not to say that you ignore your needs, but the principle here is natural and biblical: "when you do for others and meet their needs, your needs get met as well." You don't have to worry about how you're going to make it when you help others make it.

Some of the research done on peer tutoring proves this principle works in educational fields. The research showed that people, who served as tutors to others (no matter the academic ability of the tutor), increased their knowledge and improved their academic skills as much or more than the students that they were tutoring.

This smart process of doing what is best for my team every day by deliberately and intentionally pushing them up has been one of the most enjoyable journeys, and one of the most challenging for not only myself but our entire team. We currently talk about examples of what is happening in this area of our company every week. I am often walking around and hearing people asking each other, "Have you been pushed up today, yet?" and, "Who have you pushed up today?" I am continuing to learn that it is super important to put others first, because when I put others first, I usually notice very quickly that my needs and wants get met, and I get to experience an immense amount of peace and joy.

What has been challenging me and continues to challenge me is the fact that I had always been generous. I have always given to others. Growing up the way I did with Minnie Lee Higgs as my mom made me a giver. In fact, I have told people that I believe I have a DNA gene called giving. It was a no-brainer to give money, time, space, gas, loans, and basically whatever I was asked for, I gave without a second thought.

I know I wrote earlier in this book about how we grew up poor and without many resources, but that did not stop my mom from giving. One time she even gave away her tithe. She believed in tithing ten percent of her income to the church for God's work, but when she gave away her tithe, I thought; "now I don't think God would approve of mom giving away her tithe." Of course, I did not think to tell my mom this thought, but to say my mom was always giving and sharing whatever she had with everyone would be an understatement. I believe her giving beliefs lifted us out of poverty, because one day she was able to buy the house on the south side of Chicago. She purchased a new vehicle so that we no longer had to get rides to church, and we began to experience more abundance.

I believe that this is one of the most important lessons I have learned from my loss ... the value of having great human beings on the team that believe and act together because of sharing the same core values. A great by-product of our work through being rock stars is that we are not only becoming rock stars at work, but we have children and husbands and wives and relatives watching the changes that are occurring in our personal lives.

I have been pleasantly surprised and sometimes a little emotional when a team member will ask to see me personally to exclaim how working at our company has changed them and their families. One beautiful team member spoke of how she believed that she and her husband were headed for divorce court, but through our focus on these smart processes, she and her husband have a better relationship than she could have imagined before she started with us. Several team members have shared that, "I do not know what I've done in life to deserve the opportunity to work here, and I want to thank you for this opportunity."

For eighteen years I did not know how to build a team. We had great teachers and staff as evidenced by all of the comments we received from visitors, consultants, parents, and students over eighteen years, however, we were not a great team. One time in late 1999, we had a consultant visit all sixteen of our classrooms, and he came back to me with the following report: "You have sixteen classrooms functioning like sixteen different schools! No one listens to the principal. If she called for an assembly, some teachers decided that what they were doing was more important than the assembly, so they did not attend. Every teacher seems to be working autonomously from everyone else!"

While eventually we did resolve these kinds of issues, eighteen years later, we were still functioning separately instead of together like a team. I am not ashamed to admit that I did not know, and I was ignorant of how to cultivate a team. I refused to allow anyone to call us a team, because I did not believe we were a team, because I did not know what a team looked like. Again, for eighteen years, we had never been a team. We had been staff persons and employees, but not teammates.

Now, however, it is totally different. We function like we all know what our noble goal is. No, I'm not saying we're all zombies or "Yes people," without the ability to share different thoughts about issues that arise, and I'm not saying you want zombies. I am saying that what you want is to have people who believe in the same mission and vision and are willing to share the same core values so that you can train and mold your team in a way that best suits your business without a lot of infighting, major derailing disagreements, or tension in the workplace.

Our Monday and Friday team meetings are some of the most exciting times we have together as a team because we are growing and learning together as we improve, become more effective, and grow in the knowledge of what it takes to be a rock star and how we are helping each other become more of a rock star every day. During our meetings we dance and shout and enjoy each other's company as we continue to enjoy learning more about our mission, vision, and core values that are leading us to grow and expand our business every day.

If you are not at the position where you are ready with the funds and business activities to hire rock stars, no worries. When you get there, you will be ready because you will be following smart processes so that you can experience working together with like-minded people who want the same things that you do for your company.

Initially when we lost everything, a millionaire founder of another charter business out-of-state, found out about us and no… he did not give us money, but the mere presence of him traveling to visit us and to see our operations, and meet with us to hear our story was gift enough. Then for him to leave saying how he would do what he could to help us was a gigantic push up for us. We were on cloud nine for days afterward. To have someone important think that we were important enough to spend a day visiting and sharing with us the possibilities as we struggled to comprehend what was happening to our business was a great push up for us during one of our roughest times.

What About Money?

I read an article about a billionaire who claimed that always knowing his numbers helped him become a billionaire. The article did not go into details regarding just why this was so important, however, I was impressed with the fact that the billionaire focused on the process of "by the minute" knowledge of his numbers.

Absolutely you will need funds to do business. And you'll need to know the amount of funds (high or low) that you will need as you begin again differently.

However, I would like to caution you about how you get funds to do business. Is there a way you can start small without a lot of overhead? If you lost everything, like Dave Ramsey did, can you find a card table and put it in your living room and conduct business there until you get funds for an office? I think Dave's example of what happened to him is an excellent example of starting over again without any finances and being able to use what you have to get started again in business.

Dave Ramsey's story is that he began again from the card table in his living room with nothing, having lost everything except his wife and children to his bankruptcy. Dave tells his story better than I can, but the short version is that he lost everything because he had four million dollars in real estate debt, but only one million in the bank. So when his debts were sold, the new bankers looked at him being a twenty-six-year-old owing them four million dollars and decided to call every one of his loans. Because he could not pay the four million, he lost everything. After his do-over and twenty-five years later, he personally is worth over $200 million. His business does over $200 million each year in revenue, and his payroll is over $100 million. Because he believes in emergency funds due to having lost everything, he also has an emergency fund to match his payroll of $100 million just in case the economy goes bad, he will not have to lay anyone off while his business adjusts to whatever the new economic issues are.

"Well I can't do business like that—from a card table in my living room. That is so unprofessional."

Is this a thought you are having or have had? Please think about why you think that. With the virtual lives we are all living now, business is happening everywhere. A lot of business is not taking place in traditional offices anymore. In any event, I encourage you to think long and hard about where you will be conducting business as you decide your next steps in beginning again with the thought that you will want to avoid any expenses that will cause you to go into debt. Be resourceful as you look around for what you can use to get started again.

A lot of times when we think of resources, we immediately think of money. Growing up poor meant that I knew that resources didn't necessarily mean money, because we often did not have money. I had friends that had parents that were much better off then we were, but their Illinois Bell telephone services were always getting temporarily turned off due to late bill payments. My mom's phone, light bill, gas bill, and water bill very rarely if ever got turned off because even though my mom did not always have the money to pay the bills on time, she always called and spoke to customer service as soon as she knew that she would have difficulty in paying a bill. She always got extended time to pay the bill so that the service would not be turned off.

What was her resource? Her ability to be proactive was a resource. Her ability to reach out and communicate her need, and her ability to follow through on her promise of payment were resources. Every time she got an extension to pay her bill, she always had to say when she would have the funds and she always came through with her promise.

There are many creative ways to look at things differently to find resources that can help you begin again differently. Are you already in debt because of a previous business? Then you definitely do not want to incur additional debt, so looking for nontraditional resources to help you begin again differently will go a long way toward you being able to start over.

The Total Money Makeover and *Financial Peace University* are two books by Dave Ramsey that provide detailed plans for not relying on debt for any part of your personal or business lives. However, I now understand that our entire capitalism empire is based on credit, loans, borrowing, and banks. Even with this understanding, I have tried hard to avoid getting business credit cards and loans. We now own all of our equipment and property. The only lease we have is our copier lease. When we purchased copiers using cash only, it was difficult to get support for the machines because we owned the machines and the supplies, and materials and support were more difficult to get so the next time we needed copiers, we completed the lease agreement. However, next time we will do our best to make sure we don't have debt on the machines.

I also learned that it takes a lot longer to do cash transactions than credit transactions. To pay cash for large purchases has required us to have numerous conversations with vendors because they're used to, and they like it better when businesses apply for and use the credit system. This has been somewhat annoying because of the number of extra time involved in negotiating cash transactions versus credit card transactions. However, because it is a value of ours to not have or incur debt, I work hard to plan around when we need to purchase something large; we allocate enough time to make sure that we do our due diligence to not incur any debt.

Why is not having debt important? I believe once you've lost something significant like a business, having debt throws fuel on the fire. You already have lost and now you have nothing to show for your loss but a lot of debt. So going forward if you're willing to do things differently, then not having debt may need to be an option since you may still be paying off debt from the earlier loss.

I have heard many sad stories about people losing a marriage and then years later, spouses are still paying off debt that they created together. There are so many stories about woman having to change their life styles completely because they are no longer with their spouse so now, they and the children are forced to be homeless or move in with relatives due to not having enough funds

Dave Ramsey's money principles are that you utilize the seven debt-free baby steps to get out of debt so that you can build a legacy for your family by gaining wealth and doing good things with your wealth.

My motivation for utilizing Dave's principles at work was so that our company would never lose everything again, and not have to lay-off people and possibly lose our business funds and close. Dave tells a story about sponsoring a fun event for his team members and their families when his son was sixteen years old. His son did not necessarily want to be at the event, but Dave made him go for a few minutes. Dave decided to take the opportunity to help his son learn a lesson. Dave asked his son something like this, "Son, what do you see?"

His son replied, "Lots of little kids running around"

Dave replied, "I see lots of little kids who may not go to college if I, as the leader of this company, messed up and made negative headlines because I did wrong with the company's funds (or something like this) and people stopped trusting in our company and our company loss business and had to lay off the mothers and fathers you see below."

Dave explained further, "I have to make good decisions so that the people and the families that are a part of our company never have to suffer because of me and any bad money decisions I may make.

What I learned from Dave's story is that leaders have to make good money decisions or they could hurt the future lives of their employee's families.

When Albertson's Grocery Store closed down in San Antonio several years ago, many people wondered why because it closed suddenly. One day it was there and open and the next day it was closed down. Later the story came out that someone at the top of the company had made some bad money decisions like gambling and losing company funds.

When I thought about what I was hearing about Albertsons, I was very sad because I saw that an entire company went away because of some bad financial decisions made by the leadership. At the time, Albertsons had been one of my favorite stores.

Dave and Albertson's story illustrate the importance of making good money decisions so that employees and their family members don't suffer from decisions made that could potentially harm them.

By incorporating Dave's principles into the workplace, our business is on track to grow. We know that to be a business that continuously provides services to our community, we will have to focus on securing our needs without debt, putting some money each month into an emergency fund so that when business is slow, we do not have to lay-off team members, and this has propelled us to look at new and different business models that we never thought possible.

But what about if you have no money after you've lost your business? What will you do to begin again differently if you have nothing to begin again differently with? These are great questions that only you will be able to answer for sure.

I know that everyone's situation is different, and I know that you will need to decide how you move forward with beginning again differently with little or no funds. I also know that sometimes you may feel that operating without debt is not possible. And yes, I also know that not everyone agrees with Dave's principles. However, I am strongly suggesting that you take the time to reflect and review your money needs to decide your next steps.

Budgeting

One of the most important things you can do is to practice the art of budgeting regularly with the resources you currently have. By actively budgeting your current funds, you will gain insights into your priorities and wants. I believe budgeting will help you see clearly where you are financially and help you plan your future needs.

The concept of zero-based budgeting is important to review as well. When you do a zero-based budget, you budget one hundred percent of the funds you have available, and that means that is all you have to spend. If you do a zero-based budget and you are in the negative with your need to pay what you owe and also live, you will need to accept that you have an income problem. Having an income problem (not having enough funds to cover your mandatory expenses) may mean that beginning again differently may need to take a back-seat until you can get the funds you need just to live every day. I believe that your ability to think clearly about your finances will help you make the best decisions for your future.

I believe that the resources were loaned to us from God. I further believe that God's purpose for us having resources is to be good stewards of the resources we have been blessed to accumulate. People and money are important resources to cultivate and I believe as we begin again differently, we will want to think about the resources that are at our disposable so that we are good stewards and use the resources we have wisely.

Smart Process Connection from a Company Team Member:

As a new core team leader for three team members from different backgrounds and different stages in life, I reflected on the type of leader I wanted to be. Getting my team to win is one thing, but ensuring they are pushed up along the way is another.

When the agency began to focus on pushing people up, I knew I had to push up the people that were in the trenches on my team. I began to live out the mantra that "Everybody needs AIR: **A**ppreciation, **I**nspiration, and **R**ecognition." Any chance I could, I poured into my team by sending inspiring quotes, words of affirmation, and recognizing how they were excelling in our core values as we progressed along following our mission through our work.

Here are some of the comments I shared:

- "You excelled by providing the company with the detailed numbers of our project. This was a great example of using clear communication to understand what was expected of us!"
- "The way you were more than willing to step in and help the fiscal team really showed your humility and servants heart!"
- "Way to go on creating a flyer that caught my eye! You really took ownership of learning a new tool!"

Pushing up my team in this way has helped our whole team feel like they are appreciated for the work they do, inspired to continue the work, and recognized for the unique qualities they bring to the table. Pushing people up is contagious!

When creating our annual team goals, my team decided to make it a goal to push up others. On a monthly basis, each team member selects two people to hand-write a thank you note to, one on a professional level, and the other on a personal level.

Begin Again Differently (BAD) Activity #7:

Go to everydollar.com, download the free app, and set up your monthly zero-based budget. Begin using immediately or continue using your current program. Already budgeting? Begin writing in your individual growth plan (IGP) journal or spiral notebook your thoughts about how budgeting is becoming easier or harder for you. Reflect on your budgeting comments regularly to see if you are getting better at budgeting.

Current Team Member C. Ordonez's Reflection on This Process:

"I was in a meeting with Ms. Yarbrough a few months ago when she received a call from a former student from ten years ago. She took the call and enthusiastically listened and engaged in conversation with him. He was calling long distance from Mexico to San Antonio. He was going through a tough time in his life. He had been deported, lost his business, and was separated from his family. It was obvious he just needed someone to talk to give him hope. Ms. Yarbough did just that throughout their conversation. Watching the CEO of our company take time out of her schedule to listen and push him up in such a small, yet powerful way has taught me to be deliberate about doing the same in my own life."

Chapter 11:

DON'T LET FEAR STOP YOU

"Doubt kills more dreams than failure ever will."
—Suzy Kassem

Fear will be the major obstacle stopping you, but only if you let fear reign in your mind. Fear does not have to stop you, but it will if you let it. We all have fears from time to time in life. However, the power fear has is limited to what you think. Maybe you have heard the famous Henry Ford quote, "If you think you can, or you think you can't, you are right."

The power in this quote is that the focus is on the word *"you"* and what *"you"* think. It is not what someone else thinks, but what you think about you, your situation, your circumstance, your life, your nonprofit, your family, your finances… it is whatever you think, you get. So, controlling your fear becomes most important in you being able to bring your business back, re-do your business, do a do-over of your business… whatever you think will happen.

I am not saying that there is necessarily a need for us to focus on only positive thoughts all of the time. Although I think that it is a great habit to develop in order to control the fear that can be debilitating if allowed to grow and fester in our minds, thinking positively about everything may need to become a goal for us to reach for. The Bible talks about thinking about good things as a way to keep our minds from worry and fear. What I am saying is that you can control your fears by not giving into the natural fears that come with being a human with the ability to think.

Most fears are natural fears and serve to help us when we think about what can happen if we drive over one hundred miles an hour, or if we go to the edge of the cliff, or if we drink the next five after having twenty shots already. We should definitely utilize the power of fear to help us live safely. I read a newspaper story once of a young lady that had been successful in high school. She was an honor student and a star athlete, and was headed to college the next month. It was summertime and she was living life to its fullest. Some would say she had no fear, perhaps that is why they found her one-night dead from speeding down the highway at over one hundred miles per hour. When I read the story and read about her life, one of my first thoughts after being saddened by the circumstances that took her life was that she obviously had no fear. She was young, beautiful, talented, loved, and was liked by every human being she knew. She had a scholarship to college and was living life to its fullest. She had no fear and she died because she failed to have fear that driving over one hundred miles per hour could possibly lead to the car to losing control, that could lead to a crash and she could be dead.

Over about a seven-day period in April of 2019, three people died the same way in the Grand Canyon. They were taking pictures or trying to get closer to see the wonderful sites. They got too close to the edge and fell to their deaths. While this has happened throughout the years at the Grand Canyon, to have so many die within days of each other seemed to be an anomaly that could not be ignored.

I immediately thought about my recent trip to the Grand Canyon in the summer of 2018. My friends and I did a girl's trip to Las Vegas and drove from San Antonio to Las Vegas by way of the Grand Canyon. One of my friends, Rita, has grandchildren. Throughout our drive through the Grand Canyon she kept exclaiming, "I can't wait to bring my grandchildren!" She would make this comment as she would make us stop throughout the Canyon to take more pictures. I usually stayed in the car as I was driving and I do not have grandchildren, but she would jump out and immediately go to the edges to take pictures.

This worried me, and I made comments and screamed at her that I would not be responsible for explaining her death to her family, especially her husband if she fell off the cliff and died. This did not worry her one bit. Then, everyone in the car would start screaming, "Rita, stop! You're going too far! Stop, you're getting too close to the edge! Stop, that's close enough! Stop, stop, stop!" To no avail, because in our minds, Rita was close enough each time to get a picture without edging closer and closer.

Thank God she did not fall off any of the viewing cliffs where we were, but as I read the stories in April 2019, my mind went back to our 2018 trip and I began wondering if Rita would remember how we screamed at her many times to stop! Did these people fall off the cliff in April 2019 because they had no fear? I am suggesting that if they had a healthy dose of "if I get too close, I may fall off this cliff," they may be alive today. Some fear is necessary for life. In order to stay living, we must be conscious and dare I say fearful of things that could hurt us or take our lives. But the fear of not trying to re-do our business is not a fear we want to give into. Remember the movie *What's the Worst Thing that Can Happen?* This movie always allowed whatever worse thing the characters were thinking to happen to them. If they were thinking that their friend would steal their wife or girlfriend, boom, it would happen. If they were thinking that they would get caught doing wrong, boom, they would get caught doing wrong. The point of the movie was that once you think the worst, you're right, the worst will happen.

When I was raising my teenage son, he gave me a nickname of "worst-case scenario mom." At first, I did not like him introducing me this way to his friends and anyone we met. But after a while, I began to embrace the nickname because in my eyes, I needed to be a worst-case scenario mom to help him balance the natural tendency of teenagers, which is to have no fear that anything bad can happen because they think being young means being invincible.

Let us think about the fear that is normal to have and the fear that is not normal to have when thinking about starting over.

Normal fears or questions that may come to mind could be something like, "What if I fail, again? Who wants to keep failing?"

I suggest that no one wants to keep failing over and over. What about fearing the amount of work it takes to start over? You can definitely fear that the work to start over may seem daunting and you may get tired just thinking about what lies ahead of you, and the fear of fatigue, even though you haven't done anything yet, may take over. What about fearing what others may say or think as you do again what you have already failed at?

When I lost our biggest contract, I got a call from one of our Chicago board members. She rarely called me during the day unless she had questions about an agenda item for an upcoming board meeting, but because there was no meeting in the near future, I was surprised when I answered the phone and the first question out of her mouth was why were we fighting the State over the loss of the contract? She essentially asked me why wouldn't we just close because we lost our biggest contract. Fear rose up in me that maybe she was right—we shouldn't have been fighting and we should have gone ahead and closed like the other charter schools had done. These thoughts came to mind first for about a millisecond as my heart sank. I was trying so hard to not be afraid and to not worry about our situation and to have a Board Member question why I was still fighting for our business was hard for me to hear. However, I quickly gathered my thoughts and what came out of my mouth on the phone to her was a flurry of expressive "why" comments, fueled by my determination to not give in to the fear *that initially came into my mind* that maybe she was right about us fighting to stay open.

I believe I talked for five minutes without taking a breath as I explained to her about all of the parents and students we were still being able to serve, all of our past services to the community, and what it would mean to our community to still fight because they were working alongside of us in our efforts to come back and re-do and not succumb to the closing the state wanted like the twenty others that had closed before us. I rattled on and on about our mission and what we existed for until she said, "Okay, okay, I get it. Thank you!" and she hung up.

After she hung up, I slumped in my seat at my desk, super tired from the five minutes of talking I had done without breathing. I was drained, but I was super, super happy that God gave me the words to say to her.

As I talked to her and tried to convince her that there was no other choice but to fight for our nonprofit so that we could eventually have a do-over, I was really also talking to myself and giving myself some hope over fear that we could be successful again, even though it looked bad for us now. At the time, we had no income coming into our agency, and we were spending our savings on the community of students and parents who were hoping for us to get back our charter so that we could stay open. But, we had already began the work on our why for our mission work, we had started working together more as a team and we were beginning to see and realize the importance of believing and having hope. The Board Member's call to me and my response to her was really the catalyst that helped inspire us to focus on how we were beginning again differently. As we were in the final stages of losing the contract we were actually also in the initial stages of beginning again differently.

Some fear is good and necessary for safe living. Being afraid to begin again differently is also something that you may consider good and necessary. Allowing the fear to stop you is not good nor is it necessary. As you acknowledge the healthy fear you will want to have regarding finances, your faith in your nonprofit, and your hope that there is a positive future ahead if you do not give in to fear, I believe you will accept that there are great possibilities ahead for you when you allow yourself to begin again differently.

Being Honest

Being honest about whatever fears you have is a good step toward preparing for your comeback. Being able to look in the mirror and acknowledge honestly that you have no clue as to what is about to happen as you begin again can be refreshing. You can think of it like a brand-new world that you are entering.

What is the cost of succumbing to the fear that you will fail again, and why is it worth it to even attempt a do-over because of the economy or your finances or some other reason your mind can tell you?

If you decide not to attempt a do-over, or you decide that you do not want to chance it again, or if you just feel like giving up, have you thought about what giving up will cost you? As I spoke to my board member on the phone that morning, my initial fears were that she was right about questioning our decision to do a do-over and continue fighting for our business. I am so glad that I did not give in to that fear because I now know it would have been very costly for me.

Initially when we began again, we started with three staff, but now we have a $2 million personnel budget on a $12 million per year total budget. Also, four years since we started over, I now work with thirty-four wonderful team members who strive, like me, to live our mission and vision every day. One of our team members just told me that she submitted our company's name to the organization that promotes "best workplaces" for 2019. I had often in the past wondered if I should submit our agency for this recognition, but I never did because some of our eighty-three people who were not on the same page with us would have definitely provided negative comments about me and the way I was leading. When I heard my team member say that she submitted our name without asking me or telling me but just because she thought we were the best place to work, I almost cried.

Using these seven smart processes and finding integrity and other core values that work has been an amazing way to enjoy life more abundantly. When you give in to fear, I believe when you lose some of your freedom to act and think in your best interests. I further think that fear robs you of the ability to experience life to its fullest, especially in business because of our changing global economy forcing us to re-examine the world we thought we knew. By not having fear and by having assurance in knowing that by taking one day at a time we can avoid the dangers and pitfalls of fearing failure has helped me change so that I could begin again differently. You will never know what can happen when you do not allow fear to stop you from pursuing your dream of serving your community again until you change your mindset? You may never get to be famous by our world's standard, or write a book, but you can be free to be all you want to be when you do not let fear and doubt take over.

Hard Work

When you have a history of working hard you can become legitimately tired of hard work. In my case, I was in my early fifties with just a few years to go until I could pull down retirement funds. Though I never expected to retire and stop working, I did want to pull out a partial lump sum amount so that I could invest more and leave more of a financial legacy for my family. I worked hard because I had started our nonprofit in 1995 without any seed money. GoFundMe options did not exist then. I was the typical entrepreneur without a sense of day or night, and believed, at the time, that I was normal for working from sun up to sun down.

I remember hearing people say to me all the time back then, "If you forget to take care of yourself, you will not be good for anyone," but I thought I was living my dream and I loved it. I ate wrong and I slept wrong, but I was serving my community, and I believed that the important work I was doing far outweighed any concern about health issues.

Remember when Harold Washington became the first black Mayor of Chicago? I read a little bit of his story. He was intensely focused on changing the city of Chicago and improving the lives of the residents. He worked long days and nights. I read about the late-night pizza dinners as he and his team worked around the clock to implement his plans for Chicago. Then he died! Because I was born and raised in Chicago, this was very hard news to hear, but it got me thinking about my life and my work habits and my eating habits. I would like to think that I began to think differently about the way I was living; however, it would be years before we lost the contract that I was forced to change the way I was living.

Why you? There are over seven billion people on this earth and only one you. Yet you are the one facing the failure in your own life. You will be the one that makes decisions about what your next steps will be.

> *"Expect the best. Prepare for the worst.*
> *Capitalize on what comes."*
> —Zig Ziglar

Smart Process Connection from a Company Team Member:

Before I was hired and as I was going through the hiring process, I had a lot of fear. While I learned later my fear was unwarranted at the time, I was very concerned. What company invites a potential hire to a bank for an interview? I thought I was being scammed. My fear got the best of me when I started having crazy thoughts about the possibility of being scammed because the in- person interviews were scheduled to take place at a bank. Who holds an interview at bank for a non- bank related job, unless something bad is going to happen, was my thought. Of course once I got to the interview, I immediately was put at ease by the CEO, but before the interview (which had taken me two months to earn, I was full of fear). Then as a part of the final interview some two weeks later, I was invited with my spouse to a free dinner at a nice restaurant so that the YES, INC. hiring team could have one final interview opportunity with me. All throughout this process, I was excited but fearful because the hiring process was something unlike I had ever experienced. I now know that our hiring process is the most unique process that I have ever experienced or heard of. I remember thinking that the selection process was so involved and lengthy that it took longer than someone trying to get into the FBI or CIA. Most company's rush through their hiring process because they have a position that must be filled immediately. I was fearful because I did not know! I spent a lot of time worrying for what turned out to be absolutely no reason at all. People fear what they do not know. People fear what is different. Our minds wander, my mind surely did. I remember being scared to go to the in- person interview because it seemed too good to be true. I decided to lie myself into thinking I was not nervous, scared or afraid to go and needed some encouragement to take myself to the interview. I'm glad I did! The point I am making is that I took myself on a journey of a lengthy interview process and nearly made it to the final selection and because I was fearful, I almost did not go. The good news is that all of my fear went out the window the moment I was introduced to the CEO and she sat me down in the conference room and explained more about her company.

Then when I started work, I realized that the job was for real and the company was for real. What I found that was really real was that this company strives very hard to live the mission, vision and core values. I had been at companies before that had missions, visions and core values, but I had never worked for a company that actually believed enough in their mission, vision and core values to take the time to implement them across the company at all levels. While yes, it was somewhat awkward at the beginning to have hour-long meetings every week and reflective opportunities everyday to make sure I could find my connections to the company's mission, vision and core values, I began immediately to realize that YES, INC. was a special company and I was now a part of that specialness.

Today it is funny when I think back to that day when I allowed fear to overtake me in the moment. Everything she said her company was aspiring to become was true and everything she had told me prior to the interview was absolutely, positively accurate and I really had no reason to fear. Now I am changing to live more by faith and believe rather than fearing things I do not know. It really was too good and it really was true.

Begin Again Differently (BAD) Activity:

Think about this quote and write down your thoughts on whether you agree and why or disagree and why.

"Fear doesn't exist anywhere except in the mind."
—Dale Carnegie

Chapter 12:

HERE'S WHAT I KNOW FOR SURE

"If your actions inspire others to dream more, learn more, do more, and become more, you are a leader".
—John Quincy Adams

I know for sure that you now know that failing and losing happens to all of us at some time in our lives. It may be a business loss, a personal loss, a medical issue, or a marriage issue. Whatever the loss has been, you now know that there are smart processes you can begin using to help you begin again differently.

I also know that you know that all of our losses in life are different. I lost my contract, and you may have lost everything as Dave Ramsey did. Maybe you lost your dream job. Whatever your loss, you now know—and I trust and believe—that you can begin again differently to get different results.

I know that I have been able to convince you that failure is not fatal, and that if I can change and begin again differently, so can you. You will be able to rid yourself, your mind, and anyone around of the negativity that comes from thinking of failure in a way that does not lead you to success. You know that you can utilize your failures that we now call deltas to move you forward instead of allowing them to stall you and your potential.

I am convinced that we agree that having a clear vision of your business' mission; vision and establishing core values that represent you and how you want to live in this world while you conduct your business is paramount to realizing greater successes as you begin again differently.

I also believe you agree with me that the ability to stop and reflect is vital to changing into the company, business, nonprofit, job that you want, and that you can face the mirror and be okay with identifying you *"as the problem as well as identifying you as the solution"* (Dave Ramsey). You know now how powerful this conversation with yourself is towards achieving the changes you want.

We all need to be motivated and inspired, and it is great if you have an intrinsic ability to move yourself forward. You also now have some additional tools you can utilize, like the messages from Joel Osteen and Dave's inspiring story.

It is tough to talk about money when you do not have very much. But it gets easier as you see that knowing how much you have is a great start towards being able to manage more money as you grow and expand your business.

One of the main tools I hope and pray you take away from reading this book is that, when you do anything consistently, you become better at it. However, when you fail to be consistent in anything you do, you do not reap any benefits. You cannot be mediocre when making a decision regarding your do-over.

Be decisive. Did you make a wrong decision? Okay, now make another decision. Keep making decisions until you get it right.

I have no doubt that you are ready to make a decision to begin again differently. By the time this book comes out, I will be in the fourth year of our $54 million contract and the third year of our $8 million contract.

What will our company do after the contracts end? We began thinking of this very question the day we were awarded the contract in 2016. We begin focusing on working to ensure that we have an emergency fund of one years' payroll in the bank and other revenue producing services and projects to grow and expand. How long will it take us to get back up to $10 million per year ($54 million per five years) business? I do not know. This is what I do know—we are growing and expanding and doing things differently so that we will not have to lay off any of our team. We will continue to have a pot of money to share bonuses together when we knock it out of the park, and we will continue with more customers for our services. Because we are doing things differently, there is nothing but brightness in our future. Not because of some empty hope and pie-in-the-sky mentality, but because we've made decisions to do the work described in this book consistently and to continue failing forward.

I believe that once you start to begin again differently, you will begin to experience so many different benefits to life and living, even though you may be a little scared and hesitant to think that you can get started beginning again.

One of the benefits of reading this book is that now you know what you may not have known before: you know what the failure is, and you have confronted the failure so you will never fail that way again.

I am experiencing so much joy and happiness because I decided not to give in nor to give up but to begin again differently. I was willing to change. This may sound a little cheeky, but not having fear of anyone or anything that can stop me now that we have successfully done our business over is euphoric. It is an amazing joy that I can't say I can remember having at this level. Before I was living my dream, or so I thought, but now I really know how to lead more successfully, and it is so freeing, and it brings me joy. Now when I have problems, doubts, and failures, and I make mistakes, I know that I have a do-over. I know that it is okay to make the wrong decision right by making another or a different decision. When I get stuck now, I do not have to make decisions in haste. I can be okay being stuck on a problem, a situation, a decision, or anything I can just make another decision as I think through what was wrong with the first decision.

My company has been struggling for some time now with how to create a "bonus structure" to reward team members. I have read and re-read Dave's chapters in his book, *Entreleadership*, to get some ideas. I have even asked Dave's chief financial officer questions during a mastermind series I attended in Nashville, Tennessee, during a question and answer session. I was so thrilled with the answer he shared with me that day. He told me that he and another member of the thirteen-member operating board fuss and argue every Wednesday afternoon for two or more hours about bonuses and how to utilize them. I was amazed. You mean it isn't a one and done type of decision that you make and move on? You mean every Wednesday of every week for fifty-two weeks in the year, you guys argue, discuss, disagree, agree, and change to figure out bonus pay?

Now I am in my sixth month of trying to figure it out, and every time I get a new revelation about what might work for our company, I share my thoughts with our team of thirty-six, as I always practice the art of overcommunication with them to let them know where we are in the process of figuring out bonuses that compensates each of them for the excellence they are providing the company regularly. My main issue with bonus pay is that, for several years when we had our original business before we closed, most of the eighty-three people had a "negative entitlement mindset" around the concept of bonus or merit pay. I, now, take full responsibility for creating a mindset that expected bonuses or merit pay rather than being grateful for bonuses or merit pay. I realize, now, that I was not wise enough at the time to explain and demonstrate why I was or was not giving bonuses or merit pay. I also realize now that I never over-communicated any information that was difficult for me to grasp and understand. I definitely did not know how to explain my decisions regarding giving bonuses or merit pay because my decisions regarding bonuses or merit pay were not clear enough for me; therefore, I did not have the ability clearly communicate bonuses or merit pay to others.

Back then every time we received any extra funding from the State, I would give it to our teachers. Teachers who were working at charter schools usually earned significantly less than teachers working in traditional schools. In my mind, it was my duty to give all additional funds to the teachers to help equalize their pay. However, the way I told them about the funds made it seem to them that the bonus funds were owed to them. This created the negative entitlement mindset, because whenever the funds were late or less than expected, horrible attitudes and comments came from the teachers. One time I actually asked a teacher who was in my office if I could talk to her about the bonus situation. When I asked her about her attitude about the bonus payments, she replied, "Well, you told us it was our money. So why shouldn't I be able to ask why it is late or why it isn't what you said it would be?" She made this comment very matter-of-factly with no negativity but also with no signs of appreciation or gratitude.

Her comments told me that I had not communicated my expectations well and again, I realized as the messenger, it was my fault. I thought the teachers would be grateful for the additional funds, but because I set it up as an entitlement. I led them to believe that they had a right to feel like the funds belonged to them so then they could be justified if they wanted to react negatively if anything changed regarding something that they considered was owed to them anyway. I am not saying that I approve of the attitudes of the teachers at that time. I am taking full responsibility for setting up the environment that led to the attitudes because of the way I presented the bonuses.

Beginning again differently, I definitely did not want my current employees to be plagued by thinking that they were owed bonuses. I began to communicate to our current team information that was clear that bonuses are always at the discretion of the leader and whenever we had funds for bonuses, the team members would be made aware of when they would receive the bonus. However, learning what I learned from Dave's CFO really helped me to accept that I do not have to consider it a failure that I have not figured bonuses out yet. I can take time to make bonuses work for our team no matter how much time it takes. Every week now for the past six months, I have been explaining to our team where we are on getting a bonus structure set-up so that I can keep them in the loop. I really want a bonus structure that would speak to each team member and really communicate their value and recognize what they bring to the company that is helping the company grow and expand so that we never go through the loss of a contract that could destroy the company.

What does this have to do with joy? I am loving that I now know that I don't have to have all of the answers or make decisions in haste just become I'm the leader and in charge. Leadership is about making decisions and then making different decisions when your initial decisions do not work. Not going through these begin again differently smart processes may have meant that I never would have found out about the joy you get from making decisions and then making different decisions when needed.

Contentment is a great way to be and feel while going through the seven smart processes. Being able to be content with the ebb and flow of doing business knowing that you have a solid mission, vision, and meaningful core values confirm that you know that you are on the right track. If the track turns, goes over curves and through mountains and over ravines, because you are doing things differently, you don't have to give in to worry or fear. Contentment comes from not having doubt that you're on the right track. Even though you have normal fears about anything, you can be content knowing that you now have a pathway on your journey.

Experiencing success no matter what success means to you is another benefit of using these smart processes to begin again differently. You now know that you can measure success by your terms, not by society's expectations of you or anyone else expectations but your own and what you believe. The great news is that the people you select to work with you will believe like you.

Utilizing these smart processes can bring you peace even in the midst of what might look like turmoil to others. When you decide to begin again differently, and you start this journey, the peace comes from knowing that you don't have to know what the end will be, you just have to enjoy the journey towards one day at a time serving again as you begin again.

I do not want to suggest that you will have all of the answers, nor am I suggesting that you need to know all of the answers. I am suggesting that there are strong possibilities that failure is all around you, it is just a matter of time before you will fail at something again. You can and absolutely will fail again, lots of times. I now know, and you know too, that failure is not fatal nor is it final. You get to have the last word about your future. You get to chart and map out a new road for you and your company now that you know that there are strong possibilities that you will be able to begin again.

Beginning again differently does not have a time limit. I do not believe you have to hurry up and do anything that matters to you.

I do believe that you will want to allocate sufficient time and energy for reflecting and thinking throughout your process of beginning again differently so that you make the right decisions at the time that work in your favor.

I encourage you to be deliberate about setting aside a requisite number of hours each day or week to work on your business ideas as you continue to work towards regaining what you lost through implementing the smart processes described throughout the preceding chapters.

What will you do now that you have finished reading this book? Are you ready to begin again differently? Let's get started, today!

> *"You will get all you want in life, if you help*
> *enough other people get what they want."*
> —Zig Ziglar

BOOKS OUR TEAM HAVE READ, BOOKS WE CONTINUE TO READ, AND BOOKS WE ARE PREPARING TO READ AS WE CONTINUOUSLY BEGIN AGAIN DIFFERENTLY!

Jim Collins, *Good to Great: Why Some Companies Make the Leap—and Others Don't* (New York, HarperCollins Publishers, 2001)

John C. Maxwell, *The 21 Irrefutable Laws of Leadership: Follow Them and People Will Follow You* (Thomas Nelson, 2007)

Mark Sanborn, *The Fred Factor* (DoubleDay, May 2004)

Jeffrey J. Fox, *How To Become A Great Boss* (Hachette Book Group, 2002)

Kip Tindell, *Un-contain-able* (Grand Central Publishing, 2014)

Hans Finzel, *The Top Ten Mistakes Leaders Make* (David C. Cook, 2007)

Chris Hogan, *Everyday Millionaire: How Ordinary People Built Extraordinary Wealth—and How You Can Too* (Ramsey Press, The Lampo Group, LLC, 2019)

Patrick Lencioni, *The Ideal Team Player* (Jossey-Bass, 2016)

Ann Donegan Johnson, *The Value of Caring: The Story of Eleanor Roosevelt* (Values Communications, Inc. 1977)

Ken Blanchard, PhD and Spencer Johnson, MD, *The New One Minute Manager* (Harper Collins, 2015)

Joel Osteen, *Become a Better You: 7 Keys to Improving Your Life Every Day* (Free Press, 2007)

Rory Vaden, *Take The Stairs: 7 Steps to Achieving True Success* ((Penguin Group USA, 2012)

Michael Ray, *The Highest Goal: The Secret That Sustains You in Every Moment* (Berrett-Koehler Publishers, Inc. 2004)

Stephen R. Covey, *The 7 Habits of Highly Effective People: Powerful Lessons in Personal Change* (Fireside, 1990)

Dave Ramsey, *Entreleadership: 20 Years of Practical Business Wisdom from the Trenches* (Howard Books, 2011)

Dave Ramsey, *How to Have More Than Enough* (Penguin Group USA, 2000)

Books I Plan to Read Next...

Amy Dayries-Ling, DMD, FAIHM, *Solve Your Sleep for Better Health: Get to the Core of Your Snore* (Difference Press)

Dr. Francis N. Mbunya, *Skyrocket Your Business at Zero Cost: Make the Difference in Company Growth and Community* (Difference Press)

Nina Sossoman-Pogue, *This Is Not 'The End': Strategies to Get Through the Worst Chapters of Your Life*

ACKNOWLEDGMENTS

This book has been a blessing to write and to witness what happens when you utilize the power of the pen. I am still in awe that I have been blessed and chosen to be an author.

To God, thank you for giving me health, strength and a mind to want to tell my story so that I can help others the way you have helped me become the person you destined and designed for me.

To Dr. Angela Lauria, CEO and Founder of The Author Incubator for having the guts to not give up on your dream so that you could be the one cultivating me to my authorship. My life has been changed forever because of this experience.

Special thanks to Dr. Lauria's team, especially my managing editor, Cory Hott. The encouragement that he gave me was instrumental in having the right mindset to be able to finish on schedule. I appreciate greatly my managing editor, as well as everyone Dr. Lauria hired to work alongside her to change the world through helping over 800 authors like me write our books.

To my son, Benjamin, who saw me change as I was writing this book and decided to change along with me to show his love and understanding for me.

To Dave Ramsey, because I was inspired by the way he changed his life when he began again differently over twenty-five years ago, long before I knew I would have an opportunity to write this book.

To every one of the thirty-four team members at YES, INC, who worked alongside me and championed me to the finish line by showing me the deepest and most genuine love that I have ever experienced from a team of people.

To Mrs. Tiffany Warren, who was a good sport when I mistakenly thought she was my ideal reader until I realized that I was my own ideal reader.

To Ms. Cristina Ordonez for helping me read through all of the statements our team members shared about what they are learning as a part of our company and for helping me do my edit this book. You were wonderful!

To Ashley Radder-Renter for writing a wonderful foreword to this book and later helping me edit this book for publishing. You were wonderful!

To the other core team leaders who provided me with their stories about beginning again differently: Rebecca De Leon, Connie Perez, Marlene Rendon, and Brenda Waters.

To Retired Colonel Anna Rivers who knew I needed a coach before I knew that I needed to be coached.

To the memory of my mom, Minnie Lee Higgs: Her prayers are residually being answered every day for my life. Her influence is present every day in my life.

Finally, to my family and friends who through the years have made an impact on my life that led to this book being written.

Thank you to David Hancock and the Morgan James Publishing team for helping me bring this book to print.

THANK YOU

Since you've finished reading this book, I know that you are on the path to further utilizing the 7 Smart Processes to begin again differently.

I have developed a *free* class that you can take today to catapult you to the next level as you continue your journey. Email me at burteetee@aol.com to get the link to the class today. Please put this in the subject line of your email, "Send me the begin again differently link to the free class." You will receive the link within twenty-four hours.

I'm passionate about helping individuals and companies that want to transform themselves by doing things differently and changing.

Thanks for being willing to take the next step as you continue doing things differently.

ABOUT THE AUTHOR

Claudette Yarbrough is a certified teacher who holds a Bachelor of Arts degree in English language arts from the Chicago State University and a Master of Arts degree from Trinity University. She was one of the first principals to attend the Art of Leadership certificated course at Harvard University in Boston sponsored by Raise Your Hand Texas.

Her teaching career began in 1981, in Austin, Texas. She taught for six years in Austin and San Antonio before she received her Masters of Arts degree in urban studies from Trinity University.

In 1995, she founded Youth Empowerment Services, Inc. (YES, INC.), a San Antonio-based nonprofit, 501(c)(3), that helps families become self-sufficient through education. In 1998, she founded the Higgs Carter King Gifted and Talented Charter School, in which she served as a teacher, principal, and superintendent. She developed the Educator Effectiveness Process in 2010 for low-performing schools to improve their retention rate of effective educators and has since earned over $70,000,000 in grants to help schools and school leaders implement the program.

She started the Emmons Legacy Group, LLC, in 2018 to support the growth and expansion of YES, INC with a focus on helping entities learn how to win after losing. The company is named after Minnie Lee Higgs.

Claudette Yarbrough loves God and worships as a member of New Creation Christian Fellowship, a non-denominational church in San Antonio, Texas. She loves watching *Perry Mason* and *Law and Order*.

She currently resides in San Antonio, Texas, with her dog, Sally.